Even God
Rested

KIM THOMAS

HARVEST HOUSE™ PUBLISHERS

EUGENE, OREGON

Cover by Koechel Peterson & Associates, Inc., Minneapolis, Minnesota

EVEN GOD RESTED

Copyright © 2003 by Kim Thomas
Published by Harvest House Publishers
Eugene, Oregon 97402

Library of Congress Cataloging-in-Publication Data
  Thomas, Kim, 1958–
    Even God rested / Kim Thomas.
        p. cm.
  Includes bibliographical references.
    ISBN 0-7369-1027-1 (pbk.)
    1. Christian women—Religious life. 2. Rest—Religious aspects—Christianity.
  3. Sabbath. I. Title
    BV4527.T469 2003
    248.4'6—dc21   2002155126

Printed in the United States of America

03 04 05 06 07 08 09 10 11 /VP-KB / 10 9 8 7 6 5 4 3 2

For Jim

Who else but you knows where I keep myself,
and then pursues me there?

Acknowledgments

Terry Glaspey and Carolyn McCready want me to win. A writer needs to know that. Thank you.

All of my other tireless partners at Harvest House Publishers, you are the foster parents to these "children" we authors give birth to. Thank you for loving them as your own. If you didn't promote, market, and sell our books we would just be talking to ourselves. Thank you for expanding my circle.

Sara Fortenberry, you have become not only a facilitator, but a friend. I am grateful for your touch on my life. Thank you for marrying Robert and bringing him into our lives too.

Thank you, church family at The Village Chapel. You have prayed and nurtured me through another one. Most of all, thank you for loving our heavenly Father, and for learning to live "thy kingdom come" in the context of our community. You are lovely image-bearers.

I am grateful and humbled by the faithfulness of my friends. You still want to know what I'm working on and take interest in my heart. I trust you with both.

Dearest family, we are at our best in the face of challenge. God has prepared us for such a time as this, and will not leave us to bear it alone. I love how well and carefully he designed the parts of this whole.

Jim, we celebrate 25 years of marriage this June. You love, lead, and serve me in ways that continue to sustain and surprise me. Yours is the first and last face of my day—thank God for his perfect gift to me.

Contents

Spiritual Rest

"Why, I feel all thin, sort of stretched, if you know what I mean: like butter that has been scraped over too much bread…"

BILBO BAGGINS TO GANDALF,
from *The Fellowship of the Ring*
by J.R.R. TOLKIEN

Going Barefoot

*"Take off your sandals, for the place where
you are standing is holy ground."*

EXODUS 3:5

*"Earth is crammed with heaven, and every common
bush afire with God; but only he who sees takes off his
shoes, the rest sit round and pluck blackberries."*

ELIZABETH BARRETT BROWNING

Elsie is 96 years old. The Band-Aid-pink lipstick defines pencil-thin lips that arc upward at the corners when she sees me. She rarely leaves Morningside Retirement Center, but still dresses in handsomely coordinated separates and pearl earrings. Her hair is softly coiffed, unlike the tightly curled and sprayed styles of her peers. She exudes contentment. I try to sit close to her, thinking it might be contagious.

Elsie has never been married and has lived all of her life in Nashville. She went to high school barely two miles from where she lives now. And she tells me about what used to be on the corner before Vanderbilt University mowed it down and put brick buildings on it. It seems funny to me that, at 96, she doesn't tell me about all of her accomplishments or what she did for a living. In fact, after all of the times I've visited with her, I still don't know where she worked or what things made her feel significant. But when I ask her if, upon reflection, she would do anything differently in her life, she says, "Yes. I would laugh and go barefoot more."

I am not 96, only 44. Maybe there is still time for me.

I wonder why I hadn't thought of this myself. But I have been very busy trying to be very busy in pursuit of fulfillment and contentment. Too busy to go barefoot on purpose. I have been busy trying to be a grown-up, doing things and making lists of things to do, hoping that at the end of all this doing there would be a reward of some sort, one that said, "You are a really good person, and by the way, good job being busy."

As I try to consciously collect the signs that have hinted at the need for rest in my life, I see there have been many. A silent alarm has been ringing in my soul, and until recently, I have successfully ignored it. I suppose one-too-many Post-it Notes with things to do and places to be got stuck to my life. And one particularly private moment speaks volumes.

It seemed as though my husband, Jim, and I had been with friends and acquaintances for every meal during the last several weeks. I had been working until the early hours of the morning every day and getting by on just a fraction of the sleep I needed. I had written a book, painted for a one-person art show, and written and recorded an album all within the span of ten months. I was beginning to wear out, and my reserves were low. This night we were at a restaurant with six other people, and midway through the entrée I excused myself to the ladies' room. I had no actual need to go there, but some sort of subconscious buzzer went off inside me and drove me to the only place I could be alone. I shut the door to the stall, gratefully shoving the lock into place and sealing myself off from everything else. Perching myself precariously on the toilet seat, fully clothed, I put my head in my hands. Little Maybelline-brown-sable-tinted puddles collected in the palms of my hands. I let the shoes fall off my feet, and I sat there bare-foot and quietly cried.

I think that was the moment I first recognized my own need for rest, though I didn't have the vocabulary to describe it. I just knew I needed a break. I had been saying for some time, "I'm so tired," but doing anything that didn't look like work, or something not "important," seemed wrong. I felt ashamed of my desire to rest. After all, it is better to be caught doing something, anything—even poorly—than to be caught in the act of resting.

In this vulnerable pause, I heard the tiny soprano voice of a fourth-grade girl dressed in her pink Easter dress from last year: "God re-ested. God re-ested. From the wo-o-ork which He, had, done." It was the first solo I ever sang. So many years ago. No wonder I had forgotten.

God modeled rest for us. Genesis chapter two tells us that he labored for six days, and on the seventh he rested. God balanced work with rest in a healthy rhythm. He created for six days, then guiltlessly ceased from his labor. He stepped back from all of it and enjoyed, or feasted, on what he had done. It wasn't that God was so exhausted that he needed a nap. He is not vulnerable to a tiring body. But he did model for us a pattern, called Sabbath, of ceasing from our labors in order to rest. Because we are finite, we have frailties that make us vulnerable to tiring bodies. We need to cease from our own labors not only because he has modeled it, but because he designed us with the need to pause, to be restored, to rest. With the need for sabbath.

The Jewish culture today observes Sabbath from sundown on Friday 'til sundown on Saturday. They have strict rules about ceasing from labor and feasting on rest. Each household has personalized the tradition for their family in some way or another. Some gather for family meals, some do not participate in any form of commerce like shopping or eating out, some unplug the phones and televisions. They are responding to the fourth commandment of the well-known ten in Exodus 20:8-11:

> *"Remember the Sabbath day by keeping it holy. Six days you shall labor and do all your work, but the seventh day is a Sabbath to the Lord your God. On it you shall not do any work, neither you, nor your son or daughter, nor your manservant or maidservant, nor your animals, nor the alien within your gates. For in six days the Lord made the heavens and the earth, the sea, and all that is in them, but he rested on the seventh day. Therefore the Lord blessed the Sabbath day and made it holy"* (NIV).

Typically, the Christian faith recognizes the command for sabbath rest as a general principle that still applies today, but we see the actual observance differently. While practicing Jews still see it as a law to be observed ceremonially on a literal one day out of seven, the Christian tradition sees it as a law that was fulfilled in the coming of Christ. We see the distinction as much like that of tithing in the Old Testament compared to the New Testament. The principle of giving is still relevant today, but we see the specific application of the Old Testament 10 percent of our income as merely a starting place. We recognize that all of what we have is God's, and we ask for his specific leading in how to give cheerfully and generously as it applies to our life. The overriding principle is that we are to give.

The Christian ultimately finds rest in the salvation provided through Christ, but we believe that we are still called to observe sabbath rest in our daily life. Not in the Old Testament legal demand of one day in seven, but rather in recognizing that all of our days belong to God. Tilden Edwards has said in his book *Sabbath Time* that we should find a balance between surrendering to the busy demands of our culture and totally withdrawing from it. "Christian sabbath," he writes, "refers both to a special day of the week, and to a special quality of time available daily." It is in this "structural and symbolic" context that I have begun to practice sabbath rest.

Abraham Heschel describes the sabbath as the state wherein we lie still, where the weary are at rest. He speaks about how we have fallen victim to the work of our hands, and he cautions that we have neglected the pursuit of the eternal in pursuit of the temporary. This drives us to our need for sabbath rest. That is what I felt in my swirl of emotions as I sat quietly in the bathroom stall. In the busyness of all my doing, I finally stopped long enough to realize that rest is not only okay, it is essential.

The problem is that we perceive our options as either/or. Work or rest. But the reality is that life is not a one-or-the-other proposition. A healthy life finds a rhythm of work and rest that leads to wholeness. Each of us must discover this freedom.

Sometimes I work more than I sabbath because I believe that I am somehow earning extra credit with God. I must always be doing, laboring, working. I have to be reminded that God's grace, not Kim's work, has secured my standing. Christ invites me to slow down. In Matthew chapter 11, he doesn't say "Work really hard and I will love you more." Knowing the tired soul I drag around inside of me, he speaks words that pierce my heart with joy—"Come to me, all you who are weary and burdened, and I will give you rest. Take my yoke upon you and learn from me, for I am gentle and humble in heart, and you will find rest for your souls" (NIV). If those two verses, Matthew 11:28-29, cause you to exhale deeply and perhaps even weep, you are tired, my friend.

Welcome to the grace that offers rest.

For it is in this grace we can begin to practice and receive the spirit of sabbath rest. It brings balance to our souls. We balance the experiences of daydreaming and thinking, of floating and swimming, of being and doing. We engage in casual chatting and concentrated talking, leisurely reading and intentional studying. We taste the wonderful flavor of foods, and we eat for provision.

$$\sim\!\cdot\!\sim\!\cdot\!\sim$$

We have willingly looted the vaults of good sense and sacred integrity with our overbusy lives and have starved ourselves of revelation. Too much time is spent planting, and not enough smelling the roses. If what we do can't be measured in progress or dollars, we don't allow ourselves to do it. If things continue like this, it is likely we will all end up sobbing in bathroom stalls. I've discovered the need to relearn how to measure the value of starry nights, summer breezes, wonder, joy, surprise, Rodin's *La Défense,* the view from my roof, the wag of my dogs' nubby tails. Such things are best appreciated in sabbath time. Because in sabbath time, our value system changes. We find that the deeper things of life, which cost us nothing, take on a higher value. Sabbath moments give us glimpses of what is good, what is lovely, and what is God-revealing.

At specific times in our lives, we all need different types of rest. When our schedules become too demanding we recognize our need for physical rest. But on closer examination, we find that we are equally tired, if not more tired, on the emotional level. Overspending our emotional bank account, we find ourselves deeply in debt and in need of refreshment. Spiritually, we risk developing a tired faith—one that is fragile and worn out—if we take no care for sabbath rest. When you find yourself sobbing in a bathroom stall, you are dangerously close to burnout. We need all three kinds of rest: physical, emotional, and spiritual.

So how do we enter sabbath rest? God has modeled the way. On the seventh day, Sabbath, God ceased from his labor and feasted on the goodness of his efforts. This is the rhythm of sabbath rest. There are things we will need to cease from, and things we will need to feast on. Throughout this book, we'll cease and feast our way to emotional, physical, and spiritual rest. And at the end of each "ceasing and feasting," I'll suggest some practical "rest stops" for our busy lives.

God spoke to Moses through a bush that was burning. "Take off your sandals, for the place where you are standing is holy ground." Any place where God reveals himself is holy ground. Let's remember that Sabbath was the first thing God declared to be holy. He declared his work of the first six days "good," but he named the day of rest "holy." In sabbath moments, when we take the time to catch our breath, God reveals himself. And these moments are holy. So we must take off our sandals.

It seems that Elsie is right—we must go barefoot more often.

Make no mistake, learning to practice sabbath is a discipline. It requires a reordering of priorities to achieve rest. And rest is a skill that requires practice. Abraham Heschel has said that "labor is a craft, but perfect rest is an art." So I am learning to reorder priorities and schedule in sabbath time. I am trying to float often enough so that sometimes I can swim. I am taking permission to pause and rest. I am ceasing from some things and feasting on others. I am laughing more easily, and now I only buy shoes I can slip out of quickly.

Emotional Rest

"Rest is a decision we make. Rest is choosing to do nothing when we have too much to do, slowing down when we feel pressure to go faster, stopping instead of starting. Rest is listening to our weariness and responding to our tiredness, not to what is making us tired. Rest is what happens when we say one simple word: 'No!'"

MIKE YACONELLI

Ceasing from *Stress*

Feasting on *Balance*

> *"We must learn our limits. We are all something,*
> *but none of us are everything."*
>
> BLAISE PASCAL

> *"Sometimes the most important thing in*
> *a whole day is the rest we take*
> *between two deep breaths."*
>
> ETTY HILLESUM

Yesterday it iced. I'm not sure that is an official weather term, but maybe I could suggest it. "Ice" became a verb when the falling rain froze as it passed through the atmosphere. We woke up to trees with crystal glazes on them and stalactites hanging from the gutters. I can never remember which is which in the stalactites and stalagmites categories so I had to look it up again. Tree limbs bowed low from the weight, and some in our neighborhood gave up and snapped to the ground. It continued to rain throughout the gray afternoon, but the temperatures warmed. Steam rose from the rails on my balcony like wispy ballerina arms reaching to heaven.

Friends called, saying their power was out and how were we? It took a lot of discipline to say that we had plenty of heat and electricity and that they were welcome to come over and share in it. I was really in a mood to be alone. They were too, I guess. So we all stayed in our own corners. I sat cozy under a blanket on my personal chaise lounge by the fireplace in my bedroom. There was the smell of cinnamon on pine cones that I had sprayed Colonial Red and put in a silver basket for the holidays. With warm tea at the reach and dogs restraining my legs from any movement, I pulled my laptop close and began to type.

The words came in fits, and mostly stops. I tried to jump-start my word-crafting by reading some, and doing research online. I am grateful for my wireless cable modem and the flexibility of my laptop. I try to imagine what it was like to write books before computers, and before an author could do research from home the way I can. This leads me down a path of gratitude, and I indulge myself in some moments away from the book writing, to just be thankful. I'd like to say it's because I'm just a good person who remembers to pause and give thanks, but more likely it is because I am a writer who will pursue any diversion from having to really work.

When I return to my computer screen, I don't like what I have been writing. Who am I kidding, what do I know, and who's going to read my writing anyway? These, of course, are the refrains of writers everywhere. Insecurity and self-doubt always loom over my shoulder, and in less than five minutes I have moved from gratefulness to whining. The whining is a short transition time when I am basically just getting warmed up for a really good round of anxiety. I keep writing as fast as my fingers will type and don't give up until I am thoroughly wound up and hope-lessly stressed.

Personal doubts have ramped me up to thinking about unsettled decisions I needed to make but don't have time to think about because, after all, I am writing. I think about the gatherings and events I'm a part of and carry responsibilities for in the next few weeks and begin to chide myself for overcommitting as usual. My mind wanders over to my mother, who is at my sister's house in Houston recovering from a lung biopsy, the results of which we're anxiously awaiting. I start to compound my stress by allowing my imagination to think the worst, and then I begin to resent all of the things I do that aren't spending time with my family.

And not only that, I didn't go swim today because of the ice storm and so I'm sure that my stomach is growing new rolls and my rear end is turning to lard in this one afternoon away from exercising. Why did I eat cheese enchiladas for lunch when I knew I wasn't going to work out today? And where is our little church going to meet, since just this morning the broker for the building we had decided to lease called to tell us the owners didn't want to lease to a church? I begin to convince myself there are no other buildings in town that will work. The phone rings, and my publisher tells me I will need to write 5000 more words than I originally thought I was supposed to write for this book, and I see time shrink in front of my eyes. My stomach is starting to hurt, my back is cramping up, I'm hungry, and there are no low-carb snacks in the house.

Stress is consuming, compounding, and coercing my soul into the land of panic. I am grateful that at least I have naturally low blood pressure and that the sound of my heart pounding in my ears is not the precursor to a heart attack. And the most discouraging thing of all is that this is not an unusual day, except for the ice. Stress is becoming the norm for me.

And you? Have you been beaten down under relentless daily stress and commitments beyond reason? Are you worn and torn? By the end of your day are you tied up in knots trying to balance family, work, friends, finances, and life in general? Do you lie in bed in the morning wondering how you can possibly survive the coming day? It may not be much comfort, but at least neither of us is alone in this cesspool of stress.

Stress is the physical and emotional effect of life responsibilities and commitments that are out of control. And it is one of the most obvious "rest thieves" in our lives. The raw statistics show that 23 million—or one in ten—Americans suffer from some sort of anxiety disorder. At one point, the National Center for Health Statistics showed that 46 percent—almost half—of the population feels "highly" stressed. Somewhere around 9.5 million Americans see health-care professionals for stress-related problems per year, at a cumulative cost of just over $6 billion. Rashes, headaches, gastrointestinal conditions, muscle spasms, back problems, insomnia, and high blood pressure are just some of the "run of the mill" stress conditions. Add to that stress's undeniable contribution to cancer, heart disease, respiratory disorders, and suicide. It aggravates almost any other existing condition and has generated its own vocabulary of mental-health issues. And if that isn't enough, anything else the doctors cannot diagnose is labeled "stress."

It is beyond epidemic. It is becoming normal to be stressed.

Self-imposed and "other-imposed" expectations and demands we realistically cannot meet result in failed obligations and unmet goals and deflated self-esteem, not to mention irritable and frustrated mothers, wives, and employees. They give birth to a multibillion-dollar stress-related industry. For example, the antianxiety pill market is $800 million worldwide. And the publishing industry sustains huge profits in the self-help world with its solutions to stress-filled living.

Then there is the recent phenomenon of alternative medicine. It is on the grow, with profits from acupuncture, massage, and hypnotherapy—all touted to relieve stress. Some insurance companies have even begun to cover these alternative methods. Money-making gadgets and gizmos like stress balls, foam boxing gloves, relaxation tapes and videos, antistress pillows, candles, and water fountains are no longer found exclusively in specialty stores. My grocery store now offers most of those items on its regular aisles. Stress-relieving merchandise has become a normal part of commerce.

Advertising has picked up on the "stress market" and plays on our anxieties by selling us antibacterial products, implying that we should stress over the amount of bacteria in our world. We are reminded that we ought to buy mouthwash and deodorant to help cover up any physical signs of stress, and pain relievers for headaches and body aches "associated with stress."

Stress made the cover of *Time* magazine in 1985, and now, almost 20 years later, the condition commands its own section in bookstores. Beyond the simple self-help books, you can purchase targeted reading that will *make* you stressed if you weren't already. For example, there is *A Paranoid's Ultimate Survival Guide: Dust Mites to Meteorites, Tsunamis to Ticks, Killer Clouds to Jellyfish, Solar Flares to Salmonella.* Stressed yet? May I suggest nighttime reading of *The Worst Case Scenario Survival Handbook*, where you can stress over how to escape from a sinking car or survive a bear attack—just in case. So now, not only do we have to be expert mothers, wives, and professionals, but we'd better read up on these other possibilities because we wouldn't want to be caught unprepared.

I long for the simpler days when wearing clean underwear in case you got hit by a bus was the only real stress to contend with.

If you overeat or under-eat, overwork or don't have work, have a difficult job, new job, or old job, are a single mother or parent with a husband (or feel you parent your husband), have a new place to live, or a tired old place, are married or divorced, have a heartbeat or pulse, you are stressed. It is unavoidable in this life. But that doesn't mean we helplessly surrender to the inevitability of it all. If we are to enter the rest God has prescribed for us, we will have to take an occasional pause from stress.

I can suggest a few things to help you "cease from stress," and there are hundreds of books that specialize on this subject alone. But keep in mind a simple overriding principle from Psalm 46:10: "Be still, and know that I am God" (NIV). As we explore the possibilities of ceasing and feasting in order to enter a restoring rest, this is the message that must linger in our hearts. It is a call for this moment, and for this lifetime. When our hearts and minds threaten to be overwhelmed with the goings-on of the day, this watchword is the simple message that can calm us to rest.

There is no more comforting or reassuring place than the stillness that recognizes God's presence. It doesn't cause the stressors of life to magically disappear, but it begins to put things in a perspective that can lead to a more sane existence. No matter how hard we run, we can't outrun all of the "shoulds" and "oughts" that stress us and exhaust our emotional bank accounts. So we might as well sit still—and catch our breath.

May I say that in my collection of stress, it was not lost on me that, while I had just finished painting an art show, and had many responsibilities as the wife of a pastor of a start-up church, and was in the process of finishing recording a CD of hymns, and had two parents battling health problems, I had a month to write a book on the subject of "rest" and be on time for the third deadline for my manuscript.

My publishers asked me if I was writing this book because I had mastered the subject of rest myself, or if I too struggled with balancing my commitment to sabbath rest. I chortled—and gagged on my words as I struggled with the "perfectionist" in me. As much as I would like to say that these are things I have successfully mastered and practiced for years, I must tell you that I am only walking one step at a time, and am shouting to you over my shoulder the things I'm learning right now. I am one stressed and overcommitted woman, who may be just one nap ahead of you in her own pursuit of rest.

Here are three things I am learning that can help me to cease from my stress:

1. Name the stress.

2. Realistically prioritize, and eliminate what can be eliminated.

3. Retire from superwoman status.

First, put names on specific stresses. As we do this, we begin to take the power away from them to control our souls. Drowning in the unknown abyss of general stress will exponentially increase our dysfunction. So, is it overwork, unrealistic expectations, or family pressures? Are there deadlines keeping us awake at night, fears of inadequacy, or fears for provision? Could it be decisions that must be made, opportunities that must be found, or dreams that must be given up? Just give the stresses names right now—don't feel the need to begin to solve them all.

Second, try to realistically prioritize the stresses in order of intensity. This will begin to put some perspective on the panic. As you begin to recognize the relative unimportance of which clothes your child will wear tomorrow compared with the stress of paying the bills, you will actually see the stress about the clothes fall away. Context-building will make it obvious which things you are just being foolish about stressing over. And those are the things you eliminate.

Third, retire from superwoman status. This one is really hard for me. The pressure I put on myself to achieve and accomplish is beyond what any other person expects of me. I have always risen to the challenge of "extra-credit," and it sometimes costs me in the area of wholeness. And rest is not just another thing to add to my list of things to overachieve on. Ceasing from stress for me will entail a surrender of my own expectations of myself. Doing the "best you can" is not a cliché of the lazy, one to be disregarded. The "best you can" honors the image-bearer God created you to be, and at the same time it recognizes the limits and frailties of our creaturely status.

It will be important to watch for the triggers that send us back into superwoman mode if we are to successfully cease from stress. Our need to impress certain people in our life may demand that we not spend time with them while we are struggling to keep the superwoman under control. The overcommitter and perfectionist in us will crave superwomanhood, but we will have to allow those beasts to go hungry while they are being tamed.

These are all starting places. You will have to personalize your own approach to ceasing from stress. But deciding you don't want to live as a stressed person is the most important step. Stepping off the highway to a more quiet and restful way of living is a courageous move.

Someone recently told me about her friend who was in the midst of an extremely stressful period in her life. She was a working mother with all the stresses that go along with those noble efforts. Each evening when she drove home from work, before she reached her house, she pulled off the highway into a rest stop. She would take a few moments to mentally leave her work behind her so that she could, in a clear state of mind, be ready to enjoy her family and the rest offered by the sanctuary of home. She was being still and knowing.

Pull into the rest stop, and welcome your soul to sabbath rest. You are invited.

Ceasing from *Stress*

Feasting on *Balance*

*"Teach me thy way, O LORD; and lead
me on a level path."*

PSALM 27:11 RSV

*"Thus we shall always keep the depths of our souls free
and balanced, and we shall cut off thoroughly the futile
things which embarrass our hearts, and which prevent
them from turning easily to God."*

FRANÇOIS FENELON

I was on my way to swim. Most days I am singular,
myopic in focus. No turning to the left or right.
But this day, I did both. I turned right, then a
quick left, into the small congested parking lot of a local art
gallery. The yellow stripes symbolizing our uniquely American need to mark off space for "self" in our world were
freshly painted, which didn't help lessen any of the finesse
necessary to navigate the diminutive parking area.

After I secured one of the dozen parking spaces, I
tucked my gym bag into the backseat and locked it in the
car under the warm and getting-too-warm July sun. All of
the lotions, creams, and oils in my bag would expand, and

I would need to remember to be careful when I opened each bottle after my swim. Everything was going to be fine. The pool would still be wet even if I was delayed by a half hour or so by my visit to the gallery.

Allowing the guilt and pressure that I felt to fall from my shoulders, I walked the 20 paces to the door and opened it. Cool air instantly welcomed my face. I was in the beginning weeks of painting for my fall art show. This little gallery often held inspirational pieces I enjoyed examining. And I needed to be inspired. Some of the walls held oversaturated canvases with screaming colors. Those were not my favorite. There were nooks of highly decorative knick-knacks, walls with portraits and landscapes, and experimental texturized paintings. And there were pieces of artists' souls littering the entire place. I felt at home here. These were my people.

After I had sufficiently plumbed the downstairs rooms, I made the hike up the stairs to the featured gallery. Along the way, oddly juxtaposed pieces ranging from $100 to $4500 whispered for me to spend time with them. I rarely see things that interest me there, but I am always careful to look, not wanting to miss a hidden treasure. Upstairs, I am a little more self-conscious because the curator sits at his desk in the corner of the gallery. I know him, and we are friendly. But I felt bad that I was there simply to steal inspiration from the air, which he will get no commission on.

Most of the pieces I saw that day were friendly and mildly engaging. I had recently been working in wax on canvas, and I saw a piece also incorporating wax. The artist had used pastel colors and hieroglyphic figures. I examined the work closely to see how he had solved the problem of sealing the piece. (I'd sprayed layers of polyurethane on my pieces and then warned people not to allow them to bake in the sun or hang near a fireplace.) But nothing in the upstairs gallery really gripped my attention until I saw a small 5" x 7" oil painting on the back wall. I had seen this artist's work before and admired the atmospheric quality of his simple and haunting landscapes. But today, this piece spoke to *me,* not just the artist in me.

Most of the piece was composed of gossamer clouds with depth and mood, but suspended in the lower left side was a small silhouette of a little person carrying a balancing bar and walking a tightrope from one cloud to the next. The breath in my lungs slowly escaped from my lips. This was me—except I had been walking the tightrope at full speed, carrying no balance bar to stabilize me.

How long could I run full speed, precariously perched above the earth, before I would experience a fall that ended my run? How much stress could I carry and still navigate the tightrope, keeping my balance? I needed to address my out-of-control world and reassess what would be an aid in balancing me—and what would be dead weight pulling me down.

Finding a state of equilibrium in life requires that we rightly measure how much we can safely carry before we lose our footing. As we increase our stress load we usually try to hold too much, and our ability to stabilize is handicapped. A steady walk on the tightrope will mean feasting on balance.

The little man on the tightrope was using a long bar to help balance and keep equilibrium in his precarious position. I need to look at what is in my hands, perhaps letting go of some things, and gripping tightly those that would be life-sustaining.

In Exodus chapter four, a newly chosen Moses is hedging on what God has called him to do. To reassure him, God asks Moses what is in his hands. He answers, "A rod," and

God tells him to throw it down. It becomes a serpent, and Moses jumps back from it. God tells him to pick it up, and it becomes a rod again. It is only by the voice of God that the snakes we have been holding can become rods of balance to assist us in doing whatever God calls us to in our lives.

What is in your hands? Consider all of your responsibilities and commitments, and picture yourself holding them all. Can we still see your face from behind the pile? Now mentally set each thing down at the feet of Christ, one at a time. As you step back, look at all you thought you could carry. Prayerfully reach for the things you must continue to carry, for example, being a wife, mother, a growing woman of faith—and realize that, frankly, not much else is absolutely necessary. From there, ask the Lord to impress upon you which things you should invest yourself in. As you feel a peace, reach for those things and add them to your pile. This is a practical exercise that will help you put your stress load in order of priority, and perhaps help you let go of the snakes that have made their way into your hands.

When things start to go off track and explode into stress, or when what we are holding becomes a snake, the best thing to do is to throw it down. Release it. The sooner we accept that we can't control our circumstances, the sooner we can move forward. Finding a working balance for how much you can realistically carry will lead you in the paths of rest. Once you have determined what is appropriate for you to carry, you will have stepped back, ceased from your stress, and feasted on balance. You will have entered sabbath rest.

Rest is the great equalizer, balancer. As you begin to sense this new balance, it will affect which new commitments and opportunities you take on. Abraham Heschel has said that sabbath rest is the inspirer, and all else the inspired. On that day I told you of, a day when I desperately needed to be inspired, I ceased from my stressful schedule and was reminded that an unbalanced woman has nothing to offer herself or those around her. And she certainly could never take time to stop and wander in a small art gallery, where the Spirit of God had left a message for her. A small dose of inspiration wrapped in a moment of sabbath rest.

What is in your hands? Would you like to set down some of those things you are holding?

Emotional Rest Stops
Ceasing from stress, feasting on balance.

1. Be watching for your stress triggers. They can be deadlines, family conflicts, financial expenses, health issues, lack of exercise, poor communication, bad eating habits, sudden changes in plans, or poor spiritual-life maintenance. Whatever the triggers are, write them down and plan a strategy to deal with them. For example, if you know you have a deadline coming up, avoid committing to many social gatherings, freeze a pot of soup for meals, schedule "play dates" for the children during the two days before the deadline, and do anything else you can to reduce deadline-related stress. Try to anticipate instead of react.

2. What are you obsessive about? Do all the beds have to be made every day? Do all the bathrooms have to be cleaned with a toothbrush? Do the dishes have to be done every night before you go to bed? Does your hair have to be washed and "done" every day? Bring your obsessions into balance with effective compromises. For example, let me answer the four questions I've just asked with compromises:

- Get comforters instead of bedspreads so you can throw them in place instead of having to carefully fold and tuck them. Eliminate the top sheet on all beds. We learned this in a hotel in Vienna. It made making the bed a snap.

- Purchase those canisters of Easy Wipes to quickly clean sinks and surfaces in the bathroom. Keep paper towels in the bathroom for quick cleanup. Then plan to thoroughly clean the bathroom on a looser schedule.

○ Leave the dishes occasionally—just rinse them. And try one night a week with paper plates.

○ Buy a hat you look great in and use it from time to time. It gives you an option and frees you from having to do your hair every day.

3. Commit to being "good" at something *instead of trying to do* everything. It is okay to major at something and minor at everything else. I am not saying to celebrate mediocrity. But the majority of life is spent in handling the ordinary. Decide to be okay with "ordinary." We honor God when we do our best—even when we are encountering everyday, average, unglamorous opportunities.

4. Feed yourself emotionally and spiritually. A balanced life is not always about spending yourself. Take time to replenish your well.

5. Buy a tiny purse that will only hold your keys, driver's license, and a $20 bill in it. Carry it and discover how much you can do without for one day.

6. Trace the outline of your hand on a piece of paper. In the middle of the hand, write down all the things you are committed to doing or are responsible for. Hear God say to you, "What is in your hand?" As you feel led, cross off the "snakes" in your hand. Make a new list of what you feel comfortable committing to now.

7. Make a "perspective" note card. Write out Philippians 4:8 on a card that you can put near the phone, or in the car, or in your purse. Remember what is really worth stressing about, and what isn't.

Ceasing from *Noise*

Feasting on *Silence*

"Soon silence will have passed into legend. Man has turned his back on silence. Day after day he invents machines and devices that increase noise and distract humanity from the essence of life, contemplation, meditation....Tooting, howling, screeching, booming, crashing, whistling, grinding, and trilling bolster his ego. His anxiety subsides. His inhuman void spreads monstrously like a gray vegetation."

JEAN ARP

"We need to find God, and he cannot be found in noise and restlessness. God is the friend of silence."

MOTHER TERESA

I'm old now. Just yesterday I said to the waitress in a restaurant, "Could you please turn down the music?" Yep. I'm old.

I've even started picking restaurants based on the noise level as much as the menu. It seems that some have been designed for maximum noise ambience. It is as if the level of the noise is a sign of how good a time people are having. The louder the place, the more "fun" going on. I don't fit into that paradigm. I'm old.

However, I am often guilty of creating my own little noise heap at home. I might have a TV on, and Jim will have a CD going—one of us is talking on the phone while the printer churns out new information, and inevitably one of us begins to yell out something we'd forgotten to mention earlier but absolutely must pass along regardless of proximity.

But even when I am not trying to create noise, I find that I'm surrounded by unintentional noise. At any one point, my house might be filled with the noise from a dishwasher, a vacuum cleaner, the water running, the beeper on the microwave beeping, the telephone ringing, the dogs barking, the floor creaking, and the doors closing. Add to that the lifeline helicopter going overhead to Vanderbilt Hospital, a local firehouse sending out an engine, the chipper truck grinding up disposed-of branches in the alley, someone mowing or blowing a yard, and the ice-maker on the refrigerator producing its own litany of clunks, hums, and drips.

Perhaps at 44 I am more than just old. Noise does not contribute to my rest, as it overstimulates and distracts me. There is so much of it that I'm having a hard time listening for heaven. No wonder Elijah misheard the voice of God in the wind, the earthquake, and the fire. It's hard to hear a gentle whisper in the midst of all that noise.

I don't want to make the mistake of suggesting that all sound is noise. Each person has a different threshold for when sound becomes noise. My husband likes loud music in the morning. I find this horrific, and enough reason to skip morning altogether. Another friend likes to have "sounds" going at all times, whether she works or plays. I am more of a soundless individual. I would almost always prefer quiet to sound.

Some sounds can be pleasurable in certain contexts and become noise in others. Sometimes I like having instrumental music on when I am reading, but it's noise when I'm trying to sleep. The sound of my lawnmower means our lawn is being groomed—that's good, but the sound of the neighborhood mowers on a Saturday morning in full cacophonic bloom is noise. So if we are to celebrate rest and refreshment, how do we cease from all this noise?

Defining noise might help us. Most people will suffer no hearing impairment with constant exposure to an average environmental noise level of 70 dB—decibels. (Hairdryers and power tools come in at about 105 dB, to give you a perspective.) However, it has been shown that noise above 80 dB may increase aggressive behavior. And while we can tolerate occasional exposure of up to 140 dB, prolonged exposure to 85 dB or more will likely cause temporary if not permanent hearing damage. Worldwide statistics show that hearing loss from noise is one of the most common but preventable occupational hazards.

These are unarguable examples of noise. But defining it becomes more complex when we move away from just numbers and statistics and define it in terms of distraction. Sometimes noise can be silent. The onslaught of words from books, computers, signs, menus, and magazines can add exponentially to our "noise" levels.

When we consider noise in its many forms as distraction, we find four different categories: intentional, unintentional, outward, and inward. Most sounds will fall into some combination of these four. The sound of spring birds, waves on the sand, or the breeze blowing in the tops of the queen palms at my friends' beach house is not the kind of sound we are talking about here. Those "noises" are the kind we must actually listen for rather than be assaulted with.

Our culture trains us to be constantly stimulated and entertained. This is the main contributor to "intentional–outward" noise. As I alluded to earlier, TV, DVD players, video or computer games, CD players, MP3 players, boom boxes, tape decks, and radios are the main culprits here. We are either dreadfully fearful of quiet, or just plain easily bored. Whichever the case, sabbath rest invites us to cease the noise at some point for some time.

Other intentional–outward culprits are lawn tools, cars, airplanes, and even conversation. Yellers at sporting events and honkers in traffic. Fireworks, beepers, cell phones, alarms, answering machines, washers, dryers, garbage disposals, running water, flushing toilets, microwaves, heaters, air conditioners, vacuums, blowers...the list is endless. Most of these noises are associated with our need to be busy. True, things must get done, but not 24 hours a day. Surely we can "unplug" for just a while?

Almost all intentional–outward noise becomes *un*intentional when it is secondhand. Unintentional–outward noise is that which must be endured because we live in a society of more than one. So add *your* intentional–outward noise (that becomes my *un*intentional–outward noise) to *my* intentional–outward noise, and I don't stand a chance of quiet. Nor do you.

One of my pet-peeve unintentional–outward noises is the sound of cell phones in movies. If I were bolder, I would probably be a nose-puncher. When I am in the darkness of a theater and have allowed myself to be lost in a story, a phone or beeper's interrupting that bliss becomes fair game for my anger. Or talking. One time a couple just continued to chat throughout a contemplative movie my friend and I were watching. Finally, the friend I was with turned around and said, "Please...please, please, please, please, please." I would have nose-punched, but that seemed to take care of it.

When we begin to consider "inward" noise, then the subject becomes more personal. Though inward noise cannot be measured in decibels, it is perhaps the most dangerous to sabbath rest. And whether it is intentional or unintentional, it screams strongly and steadily.

Intentional–inward noise is the thing we mentally loop on. It can be anything from the replaying of our own voice—things we feel we should or shouldn't have said—to the replaying of other people's voices that have positively or negatively affected us. The most lethal intentional–inward noise is the sound of mental voices that cause us to doubt our self-esteem or our worth in God's eyes. Teachers, friends, magazines, TV, and movies are all sources of the intentional–inward noise that runs in our heads. Endless to-do lists are rehearsed in our minds, and yesterday's incomplete list speaks loudest. Hurtful words, betrayals, rudeness—they all play on relentlessly in our mind's ear. While we can unplug outward noises, we can only choose to quiet inward noises.

On the other hand, unintentional–inward noise is the stress and anxiety that we don't necessarily choose to loop on, but that assaults the quiet places of our soul in an all-out attempt to drain us of any rest. Keep in mind that unintentional is not the same as uncontrollable. We are not helpless victims of this type of noise, but it will take awareness to deal with it.

In my own experience, I have the most unintentional–inward noise in the middle of the night. I will be quietly celebrating the joys of deep slumber when I am suddenly awakened by nothing of my own doing. The longer I lay in the darkness, the more active the noise becomes. The attack will proceed progressively from fond memories at low volume to overanalyzing at medium volume to outright fear at screaming volume. And before you know it, I am fully awake and fully stressed. Sometimes, ironically, only intentional–outward noise will quiet unintentional–inward noise. So I turn on the TV and immerse myself in infomercials and old movies starring heroes from a shinier time.

What are the noises in your life? Whether they are intentional or unintentional, outward or inward, if you are to seek out sabbath rest, you will need to turn the volume down completely at some point. Sitting without on-line access or cell-phone connection will take discipline. We don't willingly give up our veneer of noise. Sometimes it is all that separates us from our fear of quiet and isolation. Someone said, "The inability to stay quiet is one of the conspicuous failings of mankind." This is a fear and failing we must overcome.

I love to swim because of the silence. The rhythm of underwater/above-water brings on a forced quiet. The intimacy of hearing my own breath and nothing else is astonishingly calming for me. Sometimes when I have my earplugs in I think I can even hear my blood moving throughout my entire body, forced from my heart to my feet by the ergonomically brilliant pumps installed when I was created. Times like this coax my soul into hungering for less noise.

I started wearing earplugs to bed at night a few years ago. I've grown so fond of them that it's not unusual to catch me with my bright-orange 30-dB eliminators in my ears when I am just sitting and reading. Or flying on an airplane. Or sitting in a restaurant.

Or trying to find a little bit of quiet between the noise.

Ceasing from *Noise*
Feasting on *Silence*

"True silence is the rest of the mind; it is to the spirit what sleep is to the body: nourishment and refreshment."

WILLIAM PENN

"Not merely an absence of noise, Real Silence begins when a reasonable being withdraws from the noise in order to find peace and order in his inner sanctuary."

PETER MINARD

The feast of silence is not one I have to be coaxed to join. I love silence. It was out of silence that God spoke all things into being. And it is out of silence that he speaks me into being each day.

It is in silence that mending takes place. It is there that discovery gives birth to creativity. Wisdom is born in silence. Peace is passed in the river of silence. It is the seed of silence that flowers into strength and courage. With all of this goodness resulting from silence, why are we so afraid of it?

In the same way that we may see sabbath rest as a burden rather than an opportunity, I think we often view silence as punitive. We see it as about what we *can't* do instead of what we *get to* do. Perhaps it is because silence

43

seems so elusive. It is abstract and uncontainable. And it is also that great abyss from which boredom gets its name.

Think of all the negative images we associate with silence. When you were in trouble, if your parents looked at you but didn't speak, it seemed worse than if they would just go ahead and lecture you. Silence from friends or potential friends always means something bad. Unreturned phone calls, the moments before a teacher calls on someone, the disquieting silence of being forgotten, and worst of all, silence from heaven in response to our prayers, all signal panic in our hearts. No wonder we have lost our affection for silence.

Jesus was not unacquainted with the sting of this silence. Before his last words on the cross, he felt the silence of heaven in a shadowing darkness unlike any we can ever know. But the same Christ who suffered the silence of the cross came to redeem, refresh, and renew all things. The silence that we may enter is not one of emptying ourselves out, but one of filling ourselves with the presence of this redeeming Christ. Silence is the time to drink deeply from his endless resources. It is a silence of body and mind, unto wholeness. Choosing silence or rest only when we are forced to by physical illness is the norm in our society. But that is not how we were designed. Silence breeds and incubates the goodness found in the remote places of our soul.

Perhaps this all sounds a bit abstract and magical. Silence is those things, but it is not unapproachable or unattainable. You don't have to go somewhere to do it, and there is no prescribed length to sabbath silence. The silence that brings rest can be found in moments or hours, alone or in community. It doesn't demand special incense or incantations—you don't have to wear a robe and make a pledge or vow. But sometimes there are "props" or tools that can help to facilitate a season of silence. Things like candles, soft light, hot baths, lovely views, and a cup of tea can lead to effective quiet.

I'd like to offer two approaches to silence which can be used separately or together. The first is a time of outward silence, and the second is a time of inward silence. While neither of these techniques is conclusive, they are a starting point. Don't wait for everything to be perfect or ideal—begin to feast on silence somewhere. Search out sabbath rest from noise.

These two approaches parallel the earlier discussion of intentional, unintentional, outward, and inward noise, and can be considered the prescriptions to the problem. First, outward silence is clearly an actual physical silence. And it can be practiced in two ways: silencing the noise around you, simply keeping a personal verbal silence, or both.

Silencing the noise around you will call for a time of coming away. It can be anything from time in the bottom of your closet for ten minutes each morning to a personal retreat where you take yourself away from your daily routine for a while. Consider, for example, turning off your radio, TV, or CD player on Tuesday mornings, when you are getting dressed for the day. Or you can silence the noise around you by rolling up the windows in your car and turning off the radio. Make a sacred time out of daily driving routines. (I recently saw this title on a book: *My Monastery Is My Minivan*.) You have to take silence where you can find it. You can set aside afternoon time for silence by unplugging the phone and plugging your ears with earplugs. Start with a "one-cup-of-tea length." Before long, you will be at "pot-of-tea length." At any point when you are tempted to break the silence, consider whether in breaking it you would call forth the goodness of God.

Personal-retreat silent times will call for planning. I have a friend who takes a quarterly retreat of physical silence. It is an unbreakable appointment he keeps with himself. He takes books to read and feed on, but he plans for a specific length of actual silence. No phones, no TVs, no CD players. He cloisters himself away to immerse himself in the gift of silence. You can do this in many ways. While it is a nice option, you certainly don't have to go to a monastery to retreat. Go to a hotel and use the "Do Not Disturb" sign. When you first walk into the room, unplug the TV and phone and radio. Make it the official act of the start of your retreat. Or maybe you can go to a friend's spare bedroom, take a sleeping bag to the garage, or even set up a small tent in your backyard. There are creative solutions for every excuse for why you can't take some time for silent retreat.

Times of your own verbal silence take much less planning. You can commit to a time of "no talking" almost anywhere and anytime. Committing to a personal verbal silence will, however, take incredible discipline if you try to maintain your normal routine. You will have to schedule appointments around it and explain to friends and family that you are enjoying a time of silence. This isn't just a game of "mum's the word." It is a time of disciplined silence for renewal and refreshment.

Now, what you do in these times set apart for silence will be up to you and the leading of the Spirit. Whether you read, or wander a museum, or take a hike, or sit in a comfortable chair and just stare at the day, the goal is spiritual refreshment. As I have said, it isn't a superstitious time of denial and emptying—it is a silence to be filled by God's presence. In the same way that the Spirit brooded over the silent waters in the beginning, the Spirit will brood over your silence.

The silence that needs the least planning but the most discipline is inward silence. Quieting the noise around you and maintaining a verbal silence will enhance the experience, but it isn't essential. It will be a matter of taking every thought captive to the will of Christ. I have found that telling my mind what to think can be challenging. The verse in Philippians chapter 4 that I use as a template for my thoughts is, "Finally, brethren, whatever is true, whatever is honorable, whatever is right, whatever is pure, whatever is lovely, whatever is of good repute, if there is any excellence and if anything worthy of praise, dwell on these things" (verse 8). This helps me to corral my thoughts and silence my anxieties. It is, again, a silence that is filled with more than emptiness. It is not simply a void—it is a time of coming away.

To those with busy schedules and family demands, the sabbath rest of silence can seem unattainable. But I am convinced that, if it weren't busy schedules and family demands, it would be opportunities and desires that kept us from silence. Or unwilling spirits and undisciplined disciples. The important thing is to set goals and try. As with any new thing you attempt, it will be awkward at first, but don't give up. We find time for anything we feel is truly important. You find time to brush your teeth and wash your face. Take those moments captive to silence. They are already disciplines at work in your life. Piggyback on them to start some new habits.

When I eat mashed potatoes and gravy, I like to make a little nest in my potatoes for the gravy to sit in. I push aside the potatoes and drop the gravy in. Silence is the tool that unhooks us from worry, anxiety, stress, and drivenness. It's the nest where God can drop things into our hearts. You just have to push aside the noise, and make a place for the silence to sit in.

Emotional Rest Stops

Ceasing from noise, feasting on silence.

1. Discover the times when you already have a natural silence in your day. Then appropriate that time for intentional silence. Consider dwelling on the attributes of God at that time each day. Use your Bible concordance to look up scriptures that speak of God's power, peace, or deliverance. Or of God as our Refuge, Healer, or Creator. Pick one thing to dwell on in that time. Remember, we are talking about filling the space with his presence, not just emptying it.

2. Build ebenezers. In the Old Testament, an ebenezer was a reminder of God's care. You could collect some stones to set by your front porch to remind you that God goes with you as you leave the sanctuary of your home each day. Plant a tree to remind you that God is your "shade" in the heat of circumstances. Draw a cross on the outside of your checkbook with a paint pen to remind you that God is responsible for your provision. These are all silent, wordless reminders that God is actively involved in your life.

3. Choose silent mornings from time to time. Listen to the sounds of life in your home and neighborhood as they wake to a new day.

4. Purchase some earplugs. I personally have a jar of 40. I put some by my bed, some in my purse, some by my reading chair, some by the bathtub. Sometimes I just wear them around the house. When I take them out, I am amazed at the amount of "unintentional noise" I have been able to eliminate with two little pieces of orange foam.

Ceasing from *Negativity*

Feasting on *the Positive*

"A cynic is not merely one who reads bitter lessons from the past; he is one who is prematurely disappointed in the future."

SYDNEY J. HARRIS

"Some people walk in the rain, others just get wet."

ROGER MILLER

"Jesus Christ never trusted human nature, yet he was never cynical, never in despair about any man, because he trusted absolutely in what the grace of God could do in human nature."

OSWALD CHAMBERS

When we moved into our present house, it was January. It was one of the coldest winters on record in Nashville, with a collection of concurrent days of subfreezing temperatures that forced us to layers and long underwear. But that didn't dampen my enthusiasm for one of our first household purchases: a hammock.

The perfectly huge hackberry tree in the backyard looked as if someone had planted it and opened it like an umbrella. The branches were multiple arms reaching for all angles of heaven. The arborist who trimmed our trees scorned my hackberry as an overgrown weed. My sophisticated response to him was, "So?" Grace and strength are not class-defined, and weeds are some of my favorite plants. And anyway, the hackberry's arms begged to hold a hammock. Even though $80 was an extravagant expense at the time, the gleaming threads of white capped by oak stretchers at the ends were not to be valued in dollars. However, because the $80 was hard to come by and would not be "come by" again soon, I wanted to secure the presence of my hammock immediately.

We drove the block-and-a-half to the neighborhood hardware store, whose owner supplied us with two appropriate lengths of chain and two padlocks. Jim and I returned to the backyard where, gloved and scarved, we began to hang and secure our hammock. As I was the high-school shortstop, the honor of tossing the chain up and over the hackberry branches was mine. We stretched the hammock from one limb to the other and locked it in place. It was big enough for two, and we began a Sunday afternoon ritual of lying in the hammock together and reading.

For nine years the hammock in the arms of the hackberry served us faithfully. The chains glistened through spring rains and winter ice until the tenth year, when orange flakes of ferrous oxide began to take it over. The negative properties of rain and time had finally caused the metal to surrender.

Rust occurs when iron is exposed to moist air over time and becomes corroded. It is an electrochemical phenomenon in which the impurities present in the iron couple with the metal. A small current is formed, and decomposition begins. The decomposed metal oxygenates, and rust is the result. In the early stages, hydrogen is produced, which slows the process. But certain bacteria feed on the hydrogen and speed up the formation of rust. The resulting destruction can be as fast as an unabated cancer. No outside agent can wreak as much havoc on iron as its own rust.

When we did some construction last year, we had to take the hammock down to allow access to the back of our house. We couldn't conveniently reach the top of one of the chains, so for the sake of speed, we just tossed the rest of the chain up and over the branch several times until it was out of the way. When I stand on my new second-floor balcony, I now look down on the branch and at the rusted chain that hugs it. I am considering leaving it there as a testimony to the corrosive results of a property turned on itself.

Negativity is an enemy to rest in our lives. It has, on our souls, the same corrosive properties as rust on metal. And while we all experience negativity, it can become self-destructive if it isn't controlled. It surfaces in our desire for things to be other than they are. When that desire becomes more aggressive and vocal, we begin to blame everything for our discontent. And we become our own worst enemies. We become a property turned on itself.

Let me list a few symptoms of negativity:

1. the twins of pessimism and cynicism

2. complaining

3. rigidity instead of flexibility

4. predictions of gloom

5. lessened sense of humor

6. jealousy

7. vocabulary of regrets and "should haves"

8. competition in even the smallest things

9. growing isolation

10. expectation of failure

Any of these look familiar?

Negativity will steal your energy and set up a stress relationship much like the one between rust and iron. Before long your soul is corroded and eaten away, and you find that you feel tired, burned out, hopeless, and unmotivated. You expect the worst. You go to a party and expect to have a bad time—be bored by the conversation, outdone in appearance, and ignored by people. Such negativity can become so devastating that you find yourself less and less able to cope with daily situations. The future seems dark and possibilities are gone. You worry more than you work to solve your problem and become immobilized in the face of the unexpected. Your verbal declarations of your own worthlessness join the collection of other self-fulfilling prophecies of failure. You continually drink from a half-empty glass.

Now, the negative person will have a tendency to give up right here. I found myself answering yes to so many of these descriptions that my shoulders actually began to slump. But if we are to enter into a fullness of rest, we must cease our negativity. Or we will find that there is nothing but rust left of our souls.

A clear beginning place would be in our talk. Negative self-talk and negative talk in general sets us up for failure. The book of Ephesians reminds us of the importance of our words. Chapter four, verse 29 says, "Let no unwholesome word proceed from your mouth, but only such a word as is good for edification according to the need of the moment, so that it will give grace to those who hear." You could easily paraphrase the first part of the verse, "Let no corrosive word proceed out of your mouth." I am not trying to say that our words are magical, like some sort of incantation or chant, but they do have an impact on us. A vocabulary that is rich in phrases like "Nothing ever goes my way," "I can never be good enough," "Why should I try?" and "No one cares" will result in anything but the edification of your soul. I'm not suggesting a childish vocabulary of Pollyanna foolishness. But an intentional effort at curbing a negative tongue is the beginning of arresting the rust.

It is possible that you do have a track record of failure, and even rejection. It is likely there are others more talented or beautiful than you are, because there is always someone who is "more" something than we are. This reality doesn't have to send us into the melodramatic pits of self-pity. A major step toward wholeness and rest will be to take a rational look at your situation and begin to see yourself as God sees you. Psalm 139 tells us that we are "fearfully and wonderfully" made. The simplicity of this statement almost obscures its power.

Sometimes when I am painting, I like to work late into the night. Because Jim is an early morning person, he will sometimes leave me to my painting and go to bed. In the morning, up before me, he will go into my studio and look at what I was working on the night before. He knows if he sees a signature on the piece, I am done with it and am satisfied and pleased that each brushstroke is as I intended it to be. In Psalm 139 David also says that when we were woven together in the womb, we were being skillfully formed, and the eyes of God were on us. We were intentionally designed. Therefore, when everything was just as the Designer intended, when he was pleased with each part, he signed his name to us in a place called soul. And he said, "It is good."

If we are to enter the sabbath rest God invites us to, we must leave the negative words and thoughts behind. That rest will be Rustoleum for our souls, and the hallelujahs for our fainting hearts.

Ceasing from *Negativity*

Feasting on *the Positive*

*"Not how we feel, but what we will, determines
our spiritual direction."*

A.W. TOZER

*"Do not be conformed to this world, but be transformed
by the renewing of your mind, so that you may
prove what the will of God is, that which is
good and acceptable and perfect."*

ROMANS 12:2

easting on the positive is a habit of mind that
determines how we will see life and whether we
will grow forward or lose ground.

A farmer discovered one day that his donkey had fallen
down into an old, dry well. After trying and failing to come
up with a way to rescue the poor beast, he determined he
would just have to fill in the well and bury the animal. With
the first shovel of dirt that fell on the donkey, she shook and
panicked at what was happening. But as she shook, she discovered that the dirt fell off her back and to the ground. And
she stepped up. This continued until, finally, the underesti-
mated donkey stepped right out of the well, having shaken
it all off and stepped up until she was back on the surface.

When life's dirt hits my back, if I am to enter sabbath
rest and feast on the positive, I have to learn to shake it off

and step up. It is the only way to gain ground toward my aim for rest. My mind will have to be convinced that I am not being buried alive by what life sends my way. So how will I set my mind in the right direction?

Feasting on the positive is not a mind-game of Pollyanna indulgence in "nice–nice," nor is it simply brainwashing ourselves with positive incantations that visualize life as we want it. Neither is it hijacking Scripture to make it support whatever "dream" or "plan" we have come up with. When I was first trying to get some of my meandering thoughts that pass for writing published, I remember being somewhat discouraged after several rejections from book companies. A Christian woman said to me, "Just remember, 'all things work together for good to them that love God.'" I think what she was saying was that a good opportunity was going to come along because God wants me to be happy. And while I appreciate that her heart was likely inclined to encourage me, sometimes this kind of thinking is wrong and builds the wrong kind of expectations in us.

Now, I completely believe what the Scripture says about "all things," and it isn't just about making me happy. It is about all things working together to make me into the woman of God that can most bring glory to him. That may come about through great publishing opportunities, or it may come about through me writing away in my little house and no one ever reading my words except me, when I read it aloud to my husband. Positive thinking doesn't mean "when you wish upon a star," it means being conformed into the image of Christ for the upward calling of glorifying God. That puts an entirely different slant on having a positive attitude, an attitude that depends on God's working in me, not my "making things happen" for myself.

Trusting that the dirt that flies around me is for my ultimate good calls me to surrender my mind and thoughts to the transforming and renewing work of the Savior who is at work on my behalf. This kind of thinking will turn everything into an opportunity. When the ultimate end is bringing glory to God, my goals and aspirations become vehicles rather than destinations. And this makes positive thinking more realistic and less narcissistic. Shaking it off and stepping up becomes a higher calling than simply trying to get through the circumstances.

This kind of thinking causes me to want to be a better, more positive woman—not so much for the sake of a healthy self-image, although that is a beneficial by-product, but because I recognize that what I am about will represent the goodness of God wherever I go. This will help me to see the dirt around me as potential planting ground, fertile ground for discovering the potential in every experience. It is this gift of transformation that helps me see the positive.

In the book of Habakkuk there is a passage that describes a failure of crops and financial leanness, and it ends by saying, "I will rejoice in the LORD, I will joy in the God of my salvation" (3:18 RSV). Habakkuk was being positive, not about his circumstances, but in the One who could ultimately bring meaning to them. It is not the dirt we are to rejoice in, fellow donkeys, it is the way God will transform the dirt that causes us to rejoice.

A story about another donkey who had her circumstances transformed is found in the New Testament. When Jesus was to make a triumphal entry into Jerusalem on what we know as Palm Sunday, he did so riding on the back of the least glamorous steed in all of Palestine. Resigned to a life of insignificant servitude, the donkey was of meager reputation. But the Savior chose her. I think it likely that when he whispered into her oversized ears, "The last shall be first in heaven, little one," she shook off the dirt and stepped up a little higher. That is feasting on the positive, enjoying sabbath rest.

Emotional Rest Stops

Ceasing from negativity, feasting on the positive.

1. What will it cost you to live in the expectation of goodness? What can it possibly gain you to always anticipate the worst, the most negative, or the most unfair possibility? Free yourself to rest by letting loose your grip on disappointment or hurt. God created for six days, and on the seventh day, sabbath, he declared it all good. Take a step toward sabbath rest and rejoice in goodness.

2. Seek to see the abundance in life, not always what is lacking. For one day, choose to eliminate all of your negative-vocabulary words and phrases—for example, "No one will appreciate all I've done," "Nothing ever turns out right," "I'm always late," "You never call me." Words are not magical incantations, but they do have value. We train ourselves in how to think by what we say. God said, "It is good"—that should be example enough for us. Dwell on the positive promises in Scripture:

- Philippians 4:19: "My God will supply all your needs according to His riches in glory in Christ Jesus."

- 2 Corinthians 1:20: "As many as are the promises of God, in Him they are yes; therefore also through Him is our Amen to the glory of God through us."

- Hebrews 4:16: "Let us draw near with confidence to the throne of grace, so that we may receive mercy and find grace to help in time of need."

- 1 John 5:14: "This is the confidence which we have before Him, that, if we ask anything according to His will, He hears us."

- Philippians 2:13: "It is God who is at work in you, both to will and to work for His good pleasure."

- Psalm 118:6: "The LORD is for me; I will not fear; what can man do to me?"

- Jeremiah 29:11: "'I know the plans that I have for you,' declares the LORD, 'plans for welfare and not for calamity to give you a future and a hope.'"

3. Search for the "frogs" in your day. What negative situations are just waiting to become princes? God wants to transform our mourning into dancing, so why not our negative "glass-half-empty" attitudes? This is very personal for me. I am a glass-half-empty girl. Because I know we live in a fallen world where things are not the way they were supposed to be, I gird myself up by anticipating the worst. But this is a self-destructive, rest-stealing way to live. I'm trying to learn to kiss my frogs.

4. Clean the rust off something you own. Lovingly remove the corrosive layer of self-destruction—and ask the Holy Spirit to do the same in your life.

Ceasing from *Numbness*

Feasting on *Sensing*

"I have no wit, no words, no tears:
My heart within me like a stone
Is numbed too much for hopes or fears...
O Jesus, quicken me."

CHRISTINA GEORGINA ROSSETTI

"I lay my 'whys' before your cross, in worship kneeling,
my mind too numb for thought, my heart beyond all
feeling; And worshiping, realize that I
in knowing you don't need a 'why.' "

RUTH BELL GRAHAM

"The great King, immortal, invisible, the divine person
called the Holy Ghost, the Holy Spirit: it is he
that quickens the soul, or else it would lie
dead forever; it is he that makes it tender,
or else it would never feel..."

CHARLES HADDON SPURGEON

Tere is a time and a place for Novocain and similar numbing medicines. But their misuse can leave you with a running nose, bleeding tongue, and drool running down your chin. Let me explain.

I get canker sores. I have friends who get cold sores, and if one has to choose, I suppose the vanity in me would push me toward canker sores because they are on the inside of your mouth where no one else has to view them. Canker sores are small ulcers that make themselves at home in your mouth for rarely less than two weeks. Typically the size of your pinky fingernail, they are angry in nature and wreak havoc on eating, speaking, and smiling. While no one has ever really figured out their cause to my satisfaction or come up with an effective remedy, it is undeniable that stress is a factor.

There have been times when I have had as many as 20 in my mouth and throat. Any scratch or abrasion in the mouth is an opportunity, so I panic if I ever bite my tongue or cheek, or chew crooked on a chip. People have given me any number of ideas, ranging from gargling with an antacid to avoiding spicy foods to taking lysine tablets. Most cures have been impotent. My little cankers live on, impervious to cure. When I have the first symptoms, I begin to growl and whimper pathetically, knowing that 15 days of torture await me.

Though I have found no cure, and nothing that really brings a shorter period of suffering, I have come upon a temporary relief from pain. There is a tiny tube of anesthetizing gel that can give me a pause from pain. It does, however, feel like acid on an open wound when applied. I have to warn Jim when I am applying it, because I stomp my feet and scream in agony. I wouldn't want him to think I was dying, only that I feel like I am.

I was taking a course in photography some years ago and was suffering with three substantial canker sores. I had two on my tongue and one on the inside of my top lip. The first meeting of my small class was on a Tuesday evening, and on that Tuesday afternoon I discovered the magic gel. After a successful application that allowed me to talk, smile, and even eat without the acute pain I was used to, I rejoiced over my golden gel. It put a protective layer of something on the sore, and it short-circuited the stimulus to the affected nerves. The initial pain was quite endurable for the net gain.

It was so effective that I put it all over the end of my tongue and top lip. I then happened to lick my upper lip, which left my outer lip and the area above it numb as well. And when I sneezed after that, I must have spread some of the gel to the edge of my nose. This left me entirely numb from my nose to my mouth, and don't forget my tongue was already numb. Sitting in the second row of desks in a classroom at Temple University on that Tuesday night, I humiliated myself thoroughly when the teacher called on me at one point. As I tried to speak up, I bit my tongue. I reached up to touch it and discovered I had been drooling and my nose was running. (This is the part where I am drooling, bleeding, and dripping.)

But because I was numb, I didn't know.

Is it possible there are some things going on in your life you aren't noticing, because you are numb? When was the last time you looked forward to anything? When did you last really, honestly enter into something and experience joy or celebration? Does life just seem dull, unintriguing? Has it lost its possibility? Have you abandoned yourself to the safety of a stoic isolation? Do you have time to feel good about your accomplishments? In fact, do you feel at all?

Overcommitted and overstressed, we become emotionally alienated from and inaccessible to those around us, and ourselves. Typically, we go along just trying to survive, and the only way we know how to do this is to shut down any possibility of feeling. With no time to feel, we live in a state of emotionally suspended animation. The layers build up over the top of our sensors, and we develop protective calluses against any outside stimulation, short-circuiting the natural response of our emotions.

You may be numb because you have endured a specific trauma in the near past. Or possibly you have been a caregiver and have needed to steel your emotions for too long. Numbness can also be a result of relationships or circumstances that have continually disappointed you and provided less than the expected results. It is also likely that increasing responsibilities and work hours have left you drained. The pressure to balance family life and work may have depleted your emotional resources, and your body and emotions have simply shut down rather than try to carry one more thing. The longer this sort of thing goes on, the more negative and cynical we become, and the less energy we have both physically and emotionally. Numbness has overcome us. We are emotionally novocained.

I find that I enter my numb state when I am either bracing for bad news or weary from just plain old empathic overload. But instead of protecting myself, by going numb I miss out on life pressing up against me. With all of its prickly edges, it is still what I was designed to encounter.

Are you drooling, bleeding, and dripping? God invites you to come and rest. Can you hear him? If not, perhaps your senses have shut down and you are hiding in the false protection of numbness. It will surely seal you off from any hope of sabbath rest.

Ceasing from *Numbness*

Feasting on *Sensing*

"The hearing ear and the seeing eye,
The LORD has made both of them."

PROVERBS 20:12

"The senses collect the surface facts of matter."

RALPH WALDO EMERSON

"Take care of your body with steadfast fidelity.
The soul must see through these eyes alone,
and if they are dim, the whole world is clouded."

JOHANN WOLFGANG VON GOETHE

I drive down this road multiple times every day. It is the main artery to my world. Going south, it will take me to the YMCA, where I try to swim four or five times a week. That same road going the same direction takes me to the mall, our favorite Japanese and Mexican restaurants, the movie theaters, our church, our neighborhood grocery store, and the local highways. The opposite direction will take me downtown and to the art museum.

Since I drive the road so often, I have subconsciously memorized the regular sights along the way. Just recently they have repaved it, and I have gladly acquainted myself with the new topography. Last night, Jim was driving us home from dinner, and I was glazing over in a twilight coma. But it is so funny how you suddenly sense when something is not as it usually is. I have a gift for that. That's probably why I can almost always find the four-leaf clover in a patch without even really trying. (It isn't résumé material, but I do take a certain pride in it.) Anyway, out of the corner of my eye I subconsciously looked down a street where some friends live to see if they were in town or not. They travel for a living. I made the mental note that their large RV was in fact parked in the driveway, indicating they must be in town. It wasn't until we were several blocks away, sitting at a red light, that it registered in my mind there had been something present I had never seen before.

Standing there at attention was a five-foot-tall gray tripod with a circular white dish on the top of it. It was anthropomorphic, a little soldier on point in their driveway. A cable went from its tail to the inside of the RV. Evidently, the little dish was collecting information from a device in the atmosphere.

There aren't a lot of satellite dishes in our neighborhood. That's probably why this image stuck in my brain and I plucked it like a four-leaf clover. Likely, my friends take it with them on the road to enhance their television reception, and maybe they were watching TV in their very own driveway that night.

Satellite dishes are parabolic in shape, designed to collect microwave signals from orbiting communications satellites. The dish reflects the information to the small metal probe in its center. The result? The receptor sends information to the television, and when they turn the TV on, it causes the RV to glow on the inside.

This process is kind of mind-boggling for a simple girl like myself. A satellite is launched into space and travels at the appropriate speed to be held by the gravity of the earth. At its speed of 600 miles an hour, it loops the earth about once every 24 hours. From its location in space, it proceeds to gather microwave signals that are then sent back to earth and collected by our little neighborhood satellite dishes.

This general process is what is referred to as "remote sensing," a term that was coined as recently as the 1950s. It describes what happens when a sensor is put at a considerable distance from a target and sends back information about that target. In contrast, close-in information-gathering is called "proximate sensing." This would be me sitting in front of my computer reading information I have gathered online. While my computer might be gathering by remote sensing, I would be receiving information by proximate sensing.

I still prefer to simply think of the entire thing as an anthropomorphic being, standing in their driveway.

Perhaps if we are to reawaken our numb souls, we will need sensory structures to gather information and light up our interiors as well. God has generously supplied us with what we need for proximate sensing. We observe the world by the agency of our five senses. We see, hear, taste, touch, and smell. These faculties become our antennae for gathering information that in turn stimulates our brains. As we use these senses, the tired and numb souls we have been living in become nourished and rested. While our senses are beautifully designed scientific wonders, they are also spiritual messengers.

Bake a loaf of bread, or pick up an unsliced loaf from your grocery store and heat it up in the oven. Break the bread open and release the goodness from the inside. The smell filling your room is the incense of yeast and flour. The aroma will sit on the cilia in your nose and work its way into the receptors, which will transmit the honest richness to your brain, where it will be identified as bread.

Then listen to it crackle as you break its crust and expose the tender middle. The "pinna," the outside portion of our ear that functions somewhat like a satellite dish by gathering sounds, will send the sound down the ear canal, causing your eardrum to vibrate. Eventually, the cochlea will translate the vibrations into nerve impulses to the brain, and you will hear the crust crackle and the faintest bit of air escape the inside of the loaf. As you hold the bread, feel the warmth transmitted from the bread to your flesh, where it stimulates nerves that send touch signals to your brain—signals reminding you it may be a bit too hot to hold very long. Then at last, tear off a piece and put it in your mouth. Let it linger on your tongue, manna for the moment, and wait for your brain to recognize the flavor and identify it as "good"—the sabbath vocabulary for total satisfaction.

Our senses are the tools to un-numb our tired souls. Revel in them. Rejoice in their enjoyment. Celebrate the *fruitio Deo*, "finding your delight in God," by entering into both proximate sensing of the world around you, and remote sensing of the God who made you.

Emotional Rest Stops

Ceasing from numbness, feasting on sensing.

C.S. Lewis says that observing nature is something we were made for. "The beasts can't appreciate it and the angels are, I suppose, pure intelligences. They understand colours and tastes better than our greatest scientists; but have they retinas or palates? I fancy the 'beauties of nature' are a secret God has shared with us alone. That may be one of the reasons why we were made."

1. Touch something. Pet a dog, a cat, a rabbit. Pet your child's head, or their smooth cheek. Touch the inside petals of a tiger lily. Then run your finger across a cat's tongue. Caress a pine cone. Feel life again.

2. Smell something. Cook with garlic, or cinnamon. Bake bread. Smell a cedar tree, wet dirt, summer rain. Swallow the aromas through your nose. Startle your sense of smell.

3. Taste something. Wash down a hot brownie with a glass of milk. Melt a breath mint on your tongue. Scrape the filling off an Oreo cookie with your front teeth. Celebrate the abundance of flavor.

4. See something. Watch a hummingbird feed. Trace a jet stream west to east. See all the varying shades of green in your grass. See the fingerprint of God on his creation.

5. *Hear something.* Listen for the difference in morning and night sounds. Put your fingers in your ears and hear your blood move through your body. Hear the bells from the local church, the alarms at the firehouse, the brakes squeal on the neighbor's car, the birdsongs. Listen for life.

Ceasing from *Anger*
Feasting on *Flexibility*

"For every minute you remain angry, you give up sixty seconds of peace of mind."

RALPH WALDO EMERSON

"Of the Seven Deadly Sins, anger is possibly the most fun. To lick your wounds, to smack your lips over grievances long past, to roll over your tongue the prospect of bitter confrontations still to come, to savor to the last toothsome morsel of both the pain you are given and the pain you are giving back—in many ways it is a feast fit for a king. The chief drawback is that what you are wolfing down is yourself. The skeleton at the feast is you."

FREDERICK BUECHNER

Remember the 1993 movie starring Michael Douglas called *Falling Down*? It was about an average American man dealing with losing his job, his wife, and his daughter. An L.A. traffic jam is the final straw that sends him raging at everyday irritants such as the cost of a soda or the quality of a hamburger. He doesn't just launch into a verbal rant—he launches grenades and smashes displays with a baseball bat. If a mild-tempered and ordinary man like him can be so vulnerable to extreme anger, what about the rest of us?

Every once in a while, I feel like I might be slowly "falling down." I can't imagine ever resorting to the extremes that Michael Douglas's character does, but I can imagine the everyday irritations of life pushing me to my limits. I find that people with too many items in the fast-checkout line at the store, and elevators that don't come when called, and catalogs that advertise things they don't actually carry in stock, and people who cancel plans at the last minute, and store clerks who know nothing about the products they sell, and fast-food restaurants that quit serving breakfast five minutes before they advertise they will, and people who don't respect the rules about swimming laps in their own lanes at the pool and the lifeguards who do nothing about it, and deadlines I rush to meet that turn out to be false, and cars that are out of gas when I am in a hurry, and rainy days when my hair started out looking pretty good, and people who talk or leave their cell phones on in movies, and wait staff in restaurants who seem inconvenienced when you ask for something, and airport security that always pulls me aside and never Jim, and running out of bleach when I am finally ready to wash a load of whites, and overnight delivery that takes two or three working days to actually show up, and running out of hot water for my bath, and things in general not going the way I planned, expected, or wanted, are some of the things that send me falling down into a fit of anger.

Anger is a personal threat to sabbath rest. The temptation of rushing full-speed into a rage-filled exploit is anything but rest-inducing. An angry, anxious, tight-jawed, clenched-stomach stance does not easily surrender to the posture of rest. Anger consumes all senses and leaves scars on all concerned.

When it comes to anger, I am a gas stove. Jim is an electric one. My pilot light is always lit, and it doesn't take much for me to go from low to high. He, on the other hand, is naturally more of a slow burn and isn't easily irritated. It takes a long time for him to overheat. But when an electric-stove-tempered person finally does get heated, it also takes them longer to cool down. We gas stoves heat up and cool down faster, all of which reminds us that, analogously speaking, each of us must find our own balanced way to deal with anger and stay cool.

I am aware that I take the world entirely too personally and that it just isn't possible that all the irritations or disappointments I experience are sent intentionally. But I can be easily convinced that someone is intentionally pushing my patience and give them a thorough tongue-lashing in my head. My mind knows the truth, but my emotions move out on the warpath anyway.

The question then becomes, if these are things that I will likely have to face on a daily basis and will have no control over, how do I want to live my life? My reaction is totally within my control. I can succumb to "falling down," or I can work toward wholeness. Living in a constant state of on-the-edge fury at everything from smudged eye makeup to misplaced keys is definitely not how I want to live. Anger is a natural and healthy emotion until it becomes rage or aggression. And that is a sharp line. Discovering how to walk the razor's edge and not bleed is the angry person's challenge if he or she is to cease from anger and drink in sabbath refreshment.

Anger is an emotional state that varies in intensity from mild irritation to intense fury and rage. There are several stages or levels of anger, typically corresponding to the respective levels of stimuli. For example, not being able to find a parking place should not produce flailing arms along with scorching words from my mouth. It is reasonable to be frustrated by not finding a parking place, but it's not reasonable to be aggressively angry.

Unfortunately, more often than not, I find I am out of proportion with my cause-and-response. It is important to find appropriate ways to assertively express my feelings without becoming aggressive. Assertiveness can be a healthy way to channel anger, if it is directed at improving the situation. Rage, on the other hand, drives us to the edge of out-of-control "falling down." There are times when fist-pounding on the bed can be cathartic, but there are other options that in the long run support a desire for rest and wholeness. I suggest four.

When we are prevented from achieving a goal, or feel unfairly put upon, or suffer uncalled for wrath from someone else, our pulse quickens and our face flushes and our muscles tense. This is the moment of opportunity. The crude evangelistic slogan "turn or burn" fits here nicely. We can either turn toward health and rest—or burn in the heat and fury of our response. The first and most practical advice for managing anger is to "pause" before reacting. This pause, even if pregnant with suppressed rage, racing heartbeat, and climbing blood pressure, is a sabbath moment that can rescue us from our anger.

Breathing in and slowing all bodily responses gives our brain a chance to shout louder than our anger and to remind us that "it's only a parking place" or "it's only words" or whatever may be the source of the irritating moment. I have found that a deep diaphragm breath inhaled, then exhaled in the silent prayer of "God help me not to overreact," has begun to lessen the potency of my instinctive anger. Placing my fury at the feet of heaven instantly brings perspective. A pause that allows you a second to regroup and voice a prayer of panic is the first tool in ceasing from anger.

The second tool is to realistically assign the appropriate level of importance to the circumstance. This is a call to perspective. Does the situation warrant exasperation and a raised voice, or is it really just not that important in the perspective of eternity? What is to be gained by my aggressive response? Is this how I want to spend myself? And sometimes, is it even worth acknowledging the irritation at all? I'm not speaking of acts of civil disobedience or nonviolent expressions of opinion. I'm talking about everyday encounters with life. Is it my job to point out the incompetence of people I come in contact with?

Rudeness, ignorance, or incompetence are not always my call to a response. Christ's table-turning episode in the temple can't be my excuse for self-indulgent rants of anger. Being the Son of God, he could see peoples' hearts and speak truth into them through the appropriate use of anger. Likely, I don't have that ability and am not spiritually gifted to turn tables. Anger at sin that results in a specific aggressive action is rarely pulled off successfully by sinners. Most irritations I allow to get to me should be shaken off and released.

For the more intense situations that call for more response, tool number three is crucial.

After counting to ten, and then trying to put the anger in perspective, the third tool is found in taming our tongues, in measuring the appropriate verbal response. Well-placed words can be effective in reducing the level of anger, just as hasty adjective-heavy responses will inflame the situation. "So…" is probably not enough of a response, but a concentrate of thoughtful words can work to deflate the situation. Deciding in advance that certain vocabulary or approaches to conversation are not options will make the response of the moment more instinctively appropriate. Words like "never," "always," "everyone," or other narrow expressions are not only not clever, they are simplistic and inflammatory. James chapter three describes the tongue as a fire-starter, full of deadly poison. The apostle reminds us that it has the potential for good and bad, and challenges us to use it for blessing rather than cursing. Wisdom would imbue our conversation with love rather than fury.

The fourth anger response tool is one that is not used in the heat of the moment. It is one that lowers our potential for wretched fury by spending our anxious energy elsewhere: exercise. I have committed to swimming this year, four or five times a week for 35 minutes each time. It is an appointment that bolsters my overall health, but it also particularly disarms my anger resources. Those who tend to be "angry people" need healthy ways to spend their overaggressive energies. Walking, biking, boxing, jumping rope, playing racquetball, and many other options for physical exertion will reduce the potential for rage. I can see tangible differences in the level of my anger on days I do and don't swim. The physical release of expending energy is a tool that silently affects my intensity level.

The mussel or oyster sits quietly on the ocean floor. When it opens its shell to eat, foreign particles like sand, or coral or seashell pieces, enter and form an instant irritant. The oyster responds to the irritant by secreting a calcium-carbonate-based fluid that covers the irritant in layer after layer of "nacre" and eventually, after some years, produces a pearl.

I suffered from an angry depression for years. For a long time, I didn't know that it was the source of my tears and despair. After some counseling, struggling, and a season of antidepressant medication, I feel much more restored. I am still vulnerable to the same angry depression, but I am more equipped and prepared. During that season, a friend told me about a book by Cornelius Plantinga entitled *Not the Way It's Supposed to Be*. In it, I was introduced to the concept of "the vandalism of shalom." Simply explained, this is the idea that peace was stolen and broken when sin entered the world. Everything God created and intended for us is not the way it was supposed to be, because of sin. I believe that this realization helped break the hold of anger and depression on me and continues to inform me of why I am so deeply angered about life from time to time. Sin leaves an ugly mark—and shalom is vandalized when I overreact in anger. But God takes my sin and vandalized shalom, the irritant of heaven, and wraps the hurt in layer after layer of his love. And pearls are born. Pearls at the great price of his son's life.

I feel certain there are pearls to be formed in our lives. By carefully responding to the irritants that come our way, we participate in the process of transformation God intended for us. Sand becomes pearl, depression becomes hope, anger becomes rest.

Ceasing from *Anger*
Feasting on *Flexibility*

"The bend in the road is not the end of the road unless you refuse to take the turn."

ANONYMOUS

"It may be hard for an egg to turn into a bird: it would be a jolly sight harder for it to learn to fly while remaining an egg."

C.S. LEWIS

"The crisis of yesterday is the joke of tomorrow."

H.G. WELLS

I have been to the dictionary. I've just come back from looking up "flexible." Aside from beginning by looking up "flexibile" (I am grateful for spell check), I found a lot of information. I did not see myself in any of the words. Sadly, the mirror became most reflective when I looked up the antonyms for "flexible": "rigid, unbending, inflexible, intractable, unadaptable, intense."

In all meanings of the word, I have never been flexible. When I was young, while other girls could easily slide into the splits, I could not easily slide into anything. In high school, I tried out for cheerleading at the end of my junior year. I worked for a whole month at being able to do a cartwheel/splits. I finally stretched my way into a cartwheel/step/splits, and even then, the skirt I wore was just long enough to hide the fact that I was a good foot away from actually doing the splits. On the day of tryouts, I tried to blend in with the other "spirited" girls. I wore my hair in a high ponytail to bring out my inner perkiness, and when it came time for me to audition, I smiled and bounced and squeaked just like a real cheerleader. But when I did my cartwheel/step/splits, I forgot to take the step in between. And in the adrenaline-filled moment, I went all the way down in the splits on a leg I had never stretched for. When I tried to stand up, my right leg shook uncontrollably, and I could not walk. I had pulled my hamstring and it was in a panic. I just sat down all alone in the middle of the gymnasium floor holding my number "14" card in front of me, and I smiled at all of the football players, real cheerleaders, and teachers who were on the judging committee. As they carried me out into the hall, I said, "I've never been naturally flexible."

I am still not naturally physically flexible. To my disappointment, I discover I am also not very emotionally flexible. The root of perfectionism that runs deep in me leads me to be intense and unpliable, and in many cases it is because of my own arrogance I think that my way is the best way. When things don't go "my way," I become angry.

Feasting on flexibility will help to deflate our tendency toward anger, and ultimately lead us to rest. When we finally realize that everything is not up to us and that our way is not the only solution to all problems, we will actually find ourselves lightening up, becoming more pliable, and on our way to being flexible.

When circumstances change or catch you off-guard, what is your first response? If it is usually anger, you must work on your flexibility quotient. When people make suggestions contrary to your plans, how do you react? Do you bristle and guard your turf? Argue for all the reasons against the new suggestions? Are you competitive in unimportant areas? Do you struggle with unpredictable outcomes? Please know that I am not saying that routines or confident and well-thought-out plans are threats to rest. But there is a subtle line that divides holding onto "good plans" from simply being inflexible. You will know when that is in your life, because anger will accompany resistance to being flexible.

Nature continues to shout God's design for flexibility in our lives. When I go out in my yard and prune my plants, I notice that the plants that are dead or dying snap off with the least pressure. The stalks that are left after my daylilies have bloomed break easily. But in the spring when I try to cut things back, when they are in the midst of their high growth season, they are so pliable and flexible that I have to intentionally cut them if I want to prune them. My forsythia bushes send out new runners, and when I try to prune them, if I don't have my pruning clippers, I have to bend, twist, and pull before they finally let loose. In the face of change, flexibility is a sign of growth, strength, and life.

When we are born, our tiny bodies are extremely flexible so they can pass through the birth canal. All of our bones and joints flex as they contort and twist their way to life. In contrast, death yields a body of stiff joints and of muscle rigidity referred to as rigor mortis.

I do not want to be a rigid person. Not only does it make me angry and tense, it prevents me from receiving rest. I want to enjoy the unexpected—to welcome change and input. I do not want to hold so tightly to who I am that I miss out on becoming who I could be. I need to retire as Queen and allow the providence of God to have more room in my life.

It is said that, for 190 million years, various kinds of frogs have been leaping around on the earth. These must be flexible and adaptable animals to have survived so long. The first thing they have going for them is that they are amphibians, so they are cold-blooded animals whose body temperature changes with the temperature of their surroundings. Some frogs dig burrows underground or in the bottoms of ponds when the air gets chilly. In this hibernation they sit perfectly still, almost holding their breath, until the warmth of spring. North of the arctic circle, wood frogs use the glucose in their blood to keep their vital organs safe while the rest of their bodies freeze solid. And Australian water-holding frogs can survive in the desert for seven years without rain by forming a sort of cocoon made of their own shed skin.

And how do we go about building this froglike flexibility into our lives? Paul encourages us in Ephesians 4 to let go of our need to defend our way and our rights. He then goes on to suggest something even harder—that we become long-suffering when we are wronged. John Chrysostom says that long-suffering is the ability to exact revenge, but choosing not to. Flexibility is born when we let go of our way, when anger gives way to long-suffering. Paul continues with a practical list of things to "put off" and things to "put on." We must shed our old ways for new. Throughout the New Testament we are encouraged to be "transformed." We are not called to these things so that we can just be "nice" people. We are called to the transforming work of Christ in our lives because of his intense love for us. And then we in turn show that love to those around us. If we are to be effective image-bearers, flexibility will be a part of our character.

Is it possible for us to become more flexible, to survive the conflicts around us by adapting more appropriately? Can I find myself surrendering my need to control in favor of relaxing in God's ultimate sovereignty in my life? And I'm not just speaking of the larger issues of faith, but the more realistically irritating so-called "small stuff" of life. Because while the trendy mantra is "Don't sweat the small stuff," I am here to remind you that the majority of life consists of the small stuff, and it makes me sweat. Can I put the small stuff in perspective and flexibly move through my day? Though it is somewhat daunting, I have more hope for these possibilities in my life than that I will ever successfully execute the splits. And I need rest enough that I will commit to those possibilities.

Emotional Rest Stops
Ceasing from anger, feasting on flexibility.

1. Allow your rigid posture to dissolve into a flexible "Gumby" approach to life and its unpredictable circumstances. Determine not to panic or fall apart when plans change and interruptions surprise you. Bend with the wind, float on it, catch it in your sail, but don't fight it.

2. What battles do you really want to fight? Do you want to dress in warrior's garb or peacemaker's? Are you being led to goodness by the anger you are tempted by? Don't poison your rest with unnecessary fury.

3. Forgive someone. Search your bitterness closet. Offer undeserved forgiveness, just as it has been shown to you by a loving Savior. It won't feel good at first, but you will get better at it. It will free you to plant something good where those roots of bitterness once nested.

Be emotional sabbath rest for someone else.

"Quietly, we are saved again."

MARK NEPO

Teach something. You have a skill that someone wants to learn. Gather with some friends and share gifts. Take turns teaching each other sewing, knitting, quilting, cooking, gardening, organizing, decorating, painting, calligraphy, wallpapering, hair-coloring.

Plant the seeds of rest in others by having reasonable expectations in relationships. Don't demand nurturing from someone who isn't good at it. Receive the gifts they offer and find a different source for your nurturing needs. Affirm the good in them, and allow them to bloom in your presence.

Physical Rest

"Our Adversary majors in three things:
noise, hurry and crowds. If he can
keep us engaged in 'muchness' and
'manyness,' he will rest satisfied."

RICHARD FOSTER

Ceasing from *Busyness*

Feasting on *Leisure*

"The really idle man gets nowhere. The perpetually busy man does not get much further."

SIR HENEAGE OGILVIE

"And so we hurtle through life faster and faster, becoming busier and busier. The result is that in our busyness we are becoming increasingly efficient at leading meaningless lives."

DON WHITNEY

"It's incredibly easy to get caught up in an activity trap, in the busyness of life, to work harder and harder at climbing the ladder of success only to discover it's leaning against the wrong wall."

STEVEN R. COVEY

How old are you when you are in fourth grade? I'm thinking 8.

I was 8, going on 44. I was a very serious child. I even had a thoughtful scowl on my face in the pictures from my first trip to Disney World. The round face located just south of my lucky beanie hat was constantly soaking in the sights and sounds around it. A second child by almost ten years, I was also independent. I confidently walked to school alone, choosing a route through the nature-trail woods, bypassing the rows of Broyhill brick houses in favor of crunching leaves and potentially undiscovered creatures. I enjoyed playing and being by myself, but could be coaxed into a rousing neighborhood game of "international spy" (patterned after the popular television show of that decade, *The Man from U.N.C.L.E.*).

Our nuclear family of two girls and a set of parents filled our suburban home quite comfortably. But sometime in the spring of my eighth year, I developed a deep desire for a dog. All of the kids in the neighborhood had dogs. A retired couple who lived behind our house had three poodles. My friends across the street had a delightful mutt named Spooky, who filled out her fur to the absolute maximum, with a coat so smooth that holding her was like trying to hold onto a small pig. Regardless of her obvious inadequacies in the looks department, she was still a pet, offering all the comforts of companionship.

I desperately wanted a dog. When all the neighborhood kids would walk their dogs, they would let me accompany them and occasionally take control of the leash.

I needed a dog.

When my ninth birthday came, in April of my fourth-grade year, my pals had obviously sensed my need. Presents and friends arrived on a Saturday morning for the party. Cake was eaten. Games were played. Needs were met.

Without my parents' knowledge, my dearest across-the-street-dog-owning friends purchased for me…a hamster. Are you surprised? Perhaps even let down? I was both. It was a lot like the year I had asked for one of those cute child-sized kitchen sets—and opened the doll-sized set Christmas morning. Or the wedding shower my friends gave me 24 years ago, when I received an amazingly ugly crystal deviled-egg holder. Sometimes we get things we didn't ask for. But what is a polite nine-year-old child to do? Embrace the hamster as her own and move on.

For days, when my neighbors would walk their dogs, I would accompany them, pulling Mr. Peabody in his cage, which was secured to my wagon with twist-ties and hair elastics.

This white albino hamster with pink eyes did not receive a welcome reception from the rest of my family. It seems he had a desire to be very busy late into the night, running on his little wheel for hours. He didn't begin this activity until the house was dark and silent, when the perpetual squeak of his wheel could have its most annoying effect. There was no distracting him from his "work" on the wheel, and so Mr. Peabody's cage was moved from the pantry, to the kitchen, to the dining room, and then to its final resting place, the garage. No place in the house was safe from the high pitched shriek of his wheel. He lived his days to run his nights. A lovely pet, but his uncontrollable busyness forced him to live an isolated life in the dark and damp garage.

Mr. Peabody lived in the garage for about a year, at which time he passed from this life due to overeating and was once again relocated. The big BFI truck took him away to his ultimate resting place.

Six months later I finally got a puppy.

Busyness can cause us to live isolated lives. We can be so busy being busy that we don't even notice when we've been moved from the pantry, to the kitchen, to the dining room, to the garage. We wake up one day to discover we are living in isolation, out of proximity from our relationships, and alone.

I don't know when it happened, but sometime during my lifetime, rest was devalued. Productivity became the most valued sign of a successful person. I'm not speaking of productivity in the healthy sense of doing good work, but productivity that has produced obsessively over-worked, overcommitted, overextended, and overspent people. No longer do we respect the person who leaves work in time for dinner with the family. They "must not want to succeed." They "aren't committed." They "aren't company people" or "management material." On the other hand, the person who neglects family and works a minimum 60-hour week is respected as the noble and honorable worker.

In our "hurry up and do" culture, we have renounced any semblance of sabbath. We live to the mantra "time is money." Even if we haven't engraved it on a plaque and set it on our desk, this is one time when our actions speak immensely louder than our words. We have traded time for money. And we didn't trade up.

The ILO (International Labor Organization) did a study in 2001–2002 entitled *Key Indicators in the Labor Market*. The report confirmed that Americans are working more hours than ever. The numbers show that the typical American worked 1978 hours in 2000, compared to 1942 in 1990s. Over one decade, Americans increased their total annual work hours by nearly one whole workweek. Only workers in the Republic of Korea and the Czech Republic worked more hours than Americans.

Terms like "human capital" and "value added per person employed" were used in the study to refer to variables in the productivity equation. Nowhere in the charts and graphs was a term shown for "rest and refreshment so you can do a better job." The spirit of the report was all work and no play.

The insatiable Gross National Product beast is fed only by the nonstop spinning of millions of hamster wheels.

And then, we can spend all of the money we have made in more nonstop activity. No longer do we have to do our shopping between the sane hours of nine and five, Monday through Friday. Now we can choose from 24-hour mega-stores, 24-hour Internet shopping access, and catalogs that have 24-hour toll-free phone numbers. We can shop anytime, anywhere, all the time. We can buy 24-hour communication with cell phones, beepers, and high-speed Internet, and never be alone. The local theater has become a multiplex, with films of all types showing at all times of the day, every day. Video- and DVD-rental stores provide unlimited entertainment in case we've seen all the movies at the megaplex. And more than 200 satellite or cable channels keep us informed and entertained 24/7 so we never have to be caught in silence.

If we succumb to the paradigm that time is money, we can never afford to not be working. Guilt and misplaced values steal our vacations. Quiet and slow dinners must be reserved for only very special occasions. Instead, fast food facilitates "doing" while we eat. We only pause when we are too sick to keep going—and even then it is likely that a nearby 24-hour pharmacy will have some chemical to prop us up enough to keep us pushing through.

And after all this wheel-spinning, what we have left to offer to those around us is an empty husk of a human being.

We have come to believe we are essential. We believe, if we don't do it, "it" won't get done. (And we also believe that "it" *must* be done.) And if we don't do it now, we'll never do it. This cycle becomes so mesmerizing that, after a while, we are doing and doing so that we can do some more so that we can get some more to help us do some more. As

Wayne Mueller says, "The wisdom of Sabbath time is that at a prescribed moment, it is time to stop." He goes on to say that if we wait until everything is finished or until things slow down, we will never find a good enough reason to stop. Soon, we will be moved to the garage.

Underneath all of this doing are buried true desires to be useful and productive. These are healthy desires. They are noble, divinely given motivations to "subdue the earth." But when taken to the extremes found in our culture, they are destroyers of shalom. It would seem that the beast we have strained to subdue has, in the ultimate coup, enslaved us. When the pursuit of the eternal is sacrificed to the pursuit of the temporary, we have traded treasure for trash. Is it possible to regain what has been lost? If we have spent more time than we have saved, can we ever catch our breath? If we have moved into the garage, can we ever move back into the house? Yes, but it will take a disciplined reordering of priorities. And the skill of "non-doing" requires practice. As Abraham Heschel reminds us, "Labor is a craft, but perfect rest is an art."

We need to change our paradigm by giving more value to the sacredness of rest. If we begin by seeing it as a part of our design, part of our spiritual DNA, we will feel more permission to enter into it and cease our running. Some of us may have to begin by putting sabbath time on our to-do list. (It is not unreasonable to "schedule" rest.) Slowly, the enforced habit will become an instinctive response. And the rest will be more restful.

Ceasing from *Busyness*
Feasting on *Leisure*

*"He enjoys true leisure who has time to
improve his soul's estate."*

HENRY DAVID THOREAU

I have heard leisure defined as the ability to
"repose without anxiety." In our American-Dutch-
Calvinist-work-ethic-oriented culture, that would
be to "enjoy time off without guilt or shame."

Perhaps a lesson from our European friends would help
us to drink deeply from this well.

Some say that Americans live to work, while Europeans
work to live. In Europe, it is accepted that the month of
August is vacation month. Long vacations, four weeks minimum, are standard operating procedure there. In 1981,
one of newly elected Prime Minister François Mitterand's
first acts was to mandate another week of paid vacation
for all French workers. This brought the total to five weeks
of paid vacation per year—in stark contrast to the typical
one week, possibly two, in America.

Because of our neglect of leisure, are we following the
path of the Japanese corporate culture? The overworked
there are literally dying at their desks to such degree that
they have come up with a term for it: *karoshi*, meaning

"death from overwork." In 1994, the Japanese government estimated the number of *karoshi* deaths at around 1000.

So somewhere between a month-and-a-half of vacation, and death by overworking, sits the sensible American. Bertrand Russell recognized our need for rest and leisure, suggesting that the last test of a civilization was its ability to use leisure wisely. We need to rewire our thinking to see the pauses in our lives to be as important as our busy times. "Busy" does not automatically equal "wise" and "important."

Every musician and every person who listens to and enjoys music respects the importance of pauses. A musical notation for "rest" instructs a pause, when there should be no note sounding. In a score, rests carry significance and importance equal to notes. In fact, intentional silence, placed strategically, sets the notes up for more pleasant presentation.

But we have come to believe that our value and identity come from what we do. Life outside of our jobs is undervalued, and perhaps looked down on, by our colleagues with a "get ahead" attitude. That can only be changed one attitude at a time. When we begin to value the rest prescribed by God properly, feelings of guilt and dereliction of duty can be transformed into feelings of refreshment, self-esteem, creativity, energy, and efficiency. Ironically, these all have positive effects on our productivity.

Sometimes, we are ambivalent toward leisure because we don't know how to "do" it. We have been too busy to put any energy toward developing our non-work selves, and the important things in our lives have been sacrificed to the tyranny of the urgent.

Can we possibly see our leisure as of equal importance to our busyness? Once we are free to say "yes," we can begin to feast. To begin to fully enjoy leisure time, some people may have to start looking at it as a job—something that is important and worthy of attention. In time, it will come to prove its worth and significance by the benefits it produces. But it will probably take intentional and strategic planning.

So, make a list. Did you ever want to learn to speed-read or keep bees? How about picking a different foreign cuisine to attempt each month? Perhaps dedicate your Saturday reading to biographies of people in fields that interest you? How about watching all the Academy Award "Best Pictures" over the next year? Or vocabulary-building or enhancing your memory skills? What would you do if you could do anything you wanted? Begin the brainstorming without interposing the filters of time, money, circumstance, skill, or the expectations of others.

When I was in grade school, my family lived outside the Washington, DC, area. We took Sunday afternoons each week after church to visit different museums downtown. When my husband and I go on "quiet" vacations (which differ from traveling abroad, when we are busy from morning to night), I try to plan ahead to bring some projects I've wanted to work on but haven't given myself permission to. I organize my recipe file, look through old magazines for ideas for my home, or bring sacks of photos that need to be put into photo albums. I used to bring along paints and canvas. Now, that leisure activity has become part of my professional life. But I never would have discovered it had I not first enjoyed it. Leisure doesn't mean the complete absence of activity. It just means activity that produces relaxation.

A young friend recently went through a relationship breakup. It came at a time in his life when he was ready to reevaluate. He felt that his world had become a fairly hollow existence of going to work and coming home. He carefully considered what he might feel passionate about, what might give him joy. So he enrolled in French classes and cooking classes in his leisure time, with a plan to study cooking in France at some point.

Leisure looks different for everyone. For many years, my professional-musician husband enjoyed reading books on theology for leisure. The vocabulary words alone were daunting to me, not to mention the tiny size of the type and the uninspired, colorless covers. But his leisure activity has led him to finish a seminary degree and now pastor a church. And ironically, he now enjoys music for leisure instead of work.

Buy a guitar, a cookbook, or a bicycle. Start swimming, walking, running, boxing, flying. Take a sculpture, gardening, music, sewing, dance, or French class. In truth, the options are endless. Once you begin to ignore the voices of "you don't deserve" and "you aren't good enough," you will begin to consider the possibilities. It all begins by recognizing that it is not just "okay" for you to enjoy leisure activity—it is essential to your well-being and wholeness. Don't wait for someone else to tell you it's okay or not okay. Honor God with the act of obedience by being his image-bearer. Cease from your busyness, and rest.

Physical Rest Stops

Ceasing from busyness, feasting on leisure.

1. Take a hot bath. Perhaps eat dinner in the tub. If the middle of the day is the only time you have for bath-taking, do it then. Play music you enjoy. Read a magazine or a book. Fill the tub with bubbles or bath salts that change the color of the water.

2. Shop for one luxury item. Set a budget. If it is $25, feel the freedom to spend it however you want to. A special meal out by yourself, three desserts, a tube of expensive lipstick, or five tubes of cheap lipstick.

3. Look through old photos with no goal of organizing them. Just enjoy them and relive the memories.

4. Read some chapters in a book you've been wanting to read. Determine at the outset how many chapters you are going to read, and then do it in total freedom.

5. Try a new recipe with no fear of failing. You can always order pizza.

6. Enjoy seasons of fasting—from buying things, from TV, radio, books, telephone, computer, the Internet. Use your hour of fasting every week to do something you've been needing to do. For example, clean out a cabinet, organize the bills, write letters, mend something. The fast, followed by accomplishment, will produce a restful refreshment.

7. Wander in an art museum. If you aren't artistically inclined, pick something specific to look for in the paintings. For example, make a note of everything that is painted red. Or note how the eyes are painted in each painting. Give names to the people. Suddenly you will be lost in a new adventure.

8. And then, experiment with a new hobby. Buy a canvas no smaller than 16 x 20. Set up a still life to paint from, or follow a photograph, or copy a great master's painting, or make it up as you go. Don't quit until you have finished and have painted all the way to the edges of the canvas.

9. Bake and decorate sugar cookies. One Christmas, I took one cookie cutter, two bottles of colored sugar, and a sugar-cookie recipe home to my parents' house. We mixed up the dough and rolled it out, then everyone took turns decorating the cookies. One ended up with raisin eyes, one became a wheel with almond spokes, and one strongly resembled a disagreeable political figure. What is "baking" in your sabbath rest time?

10. Do something physical. We need a physical release from pressure from time to time if we are to really rest. Go bowling, roller-skate, hike, scrub walls or clean windows, jump rope, dance through the house. Fly a kite, shoot some baskets, ride a bike. Swim, water-jog, lift weights. Spend some energy in a leisurely atmosphere, with no other agenda.

11. Create something. Go to one of those pottery places where you can make a mug, or a plate, or a bowl. Make up a pasta dish for dinner with whatever is in the pantry. If your hair is straight, curl it. If it is curly, straighten it. Plan a garden. Make a pillow with colors you find restful.

Cut out pictures from travel magazines of places you would like to go and glue them onto postcards. Use them for "thinking of you" notes.

Try this drawing experiment (you do not have to be talented to experience creating something): Draw a picture of your house as viewed from the street. Then draw it with your other hand. Then put the pencil point in contact with the paper and don't pick it up until you have finished drawing the outline of the house. Then hold the pencil by its very end and draw the house. Finally, draw it again with your original hand. Notice the character of line in this piece compared to the first one. You may find the latent artist in you that hasn't had time to surface.

12. Play. Splash in mud puddles on a rainy day, make up a song about driving to wherever you are going, jump on your bed, build a castle out of your mashed potatoes, get sidewalk chalk and draw on your front sidewalk, collect fireflies in a jar, lie down in the grass and see cloud pictures, ride a merry-go-round.

Ceasing from *Hurrying*

Feasting on *Slowing Down*

*"Now here, you see, it takes all the running you can do,
to keep in the same place. If you want to get somewhere
else, you must run at least twice as fast as that!"*

LEWIS CARROLL

"Make haste slowly."

AUGUSTUS CAESAR

I recently saw an article in a magazine entitled
"Relax in a Hurry." The description said, "Mini
relaxation exercises help reduce anxiety and tension immediately!" This makes me tense. Do we even have
to relax fast?

It seems that we are constantly answering to the little
voice in our heads that says "faster, faster, faster!" Of course,
we must do things fast and in a hurry if we are to save
time. As if saving time was even possible. Problem is, you
cannot save hours from today to apply to tomorrow. Every
24 hours the restart button is pushed. It's as if I tried to
breathe a lot of extra breaths today so I wouldn't have to
be bothered with that nuisance tomorrow.

⁓ · ⁓ · ⁓

Were you late for anything today? Did you rush down a
meal? Did you exceed the speed limit, complain about a

slow line, multitask in some way, or upgrade anything to the newer, faster version? Have you forgotten appointments or misplaced things? Do you have windburn from the speed at which you ran through your day? If you said yes at all, you are, like most of us, a "hurrier."

Recently, I forgot to put any undergarments in my gym bag for after my swim. When I realized I had forgotten said items, I actually thought to myself, *Well, that will save me some time when I'm getting dressed.* I am a perpetual hurrier, declaring myself the victor for each minute saved. I am a hurrier even when there's no good reason. Is it really necessary to be first off the line at every red light? Have I saved up a lot of time from all the elevator rides during which I've pushed the "close door" button over and over? And how much time am I really gaining by cutting through the Krystal Hamburger lot instead of waiting at the red light at the intersection of Hillsboro Road and Abbott Martin? Oh, how very clever I am.

I can't think of the last Sunday morning when we drove to church leisurely, with time to linger and enjoy the view. Instead, I usually rush out the door, lucky to have matching shoes on, only to discover I have forgotten my Bible. Harried and grumpy, I rush in to get a good seat and thrash my way through worship.

I love to see movies. I've missed many a preview, even opening scene. And I know I should allow extra time, but it really irritates me when I get to the multiplex and discover that only two of the eight ticket lines are open, and only one of the concession lines. They may have designed for speed, but they have not staffed for it. Now that just isn't right in my hurry-up world.

I get really frustrated by people in the left-turn lane who won't go until the light turns red. Or people who have 30 items in the 15-or-under line. Or teenagers who stroll across the street in front of me, showing no sense of urgency at all. Or Web sites that don't download quickly. I am addicted to a McLife: fast and cheap and on my way.

I am guilty of hurry. And it threatens to steal any tiny plot of ground surrendered to sabbath rest. Gandhi said, "There is more to life than merely increasing its speed." We need to slow down to the speed of life.

So what is the speed of life? Well, gestation for human life is nine months. I suppose for the African elephant that seems rushed, as its gestation period is just shy of two years. Yet the little deer mouse carries its young for only three weeks. Each of these times is intricately designed for the appropriate speed of life. The earth takes 365 days, 5 hours, 48 minutes, and 45.51 seconds to make one complete revolution around the sun. And the earth completes one rotation on its axis every 24 hours. To everything, a time. None is to be hurried or rushed, or all of life is thrown off.

Slipping back into the speed of life will mean stopping the hurry. Practically speaking, that means we'll need to cease from overcommitting and procrastinating. It is likely that one of these two habits is what sends us into overdrive most days, and a combination of both boosts us into an unlivable high-speed race against sundown every day.

The overcommitter must simply do less. But before we can choose to do less, we must recognize exactly what an overcommitter looks like. She is likely an overachiever with a limited ability to use the word "no" or say "yes" to personal wellness. And aside from her perfectionist tendencies, she is probably a people-pleaser. In the short run, these things make her a good friend, daughter, mother, and wife, but often at the expense of her own wholeness. Do you accept more responsibilities when your list is actually quite full? Do you feel better about yourself when others are counting on you? Would you rather do it yourself than ask someone to help? Do you think people who say "no" are probably self-consumed narcissists? If you said yes to any of these, you are an overcommitter.

I know. I not only write about it—I am one.

⁓ · ⌣ · ⁓

We overcommitters will find great freedom when we begin to assess time with a more realistic view to what we can reasonably accomplish. I seem to have only two speeds: fast and stop. If I have two things to do in a day, I probably won't get either done. But if I have a dozen or more things, I'll get two dozen done. I thrive on the flurry and adrenaline of busyness. But a lifetime lived this way will spread us too thin and spend us too dry, and will end up costing us or those around us. The race that begins with hurrying up so we can save time often ends with us too tired and spent to even think of a way to enjoy the extra time. The speed of life urges us to not go faster, but to become reconciled with an appropriate pace.

There are several questions that the overcommitter can begin to ask. First, am I responding to something that really needs to be done, or am I responding to my need for approval? A healthy self-esteem that practices seeing through the eyes of God will eliminate some of these over-commitments. God's love and acceptance do not depend on what I do. His grace is not opposed to my efforts, but my efforts do not earn his grace.

Next, the overcommitter must ask, is this something urgent or important that I am committing to? The urgent will always consume the overcommitter at the expense of the truly important. A studied reordering of priorities, with particular attention to what is ultimately important, will help us weed the unnecessary out of our lists.

And lastly, the overcommitter should try to assess what can reasonably be accomplished in the time set before him or her. Likely, whatever the answer, the overcommitter should drop two more things from the list. We always think we can squeeze more than 60 minutes from an hour, but the physics of time will work against us without fail.

So what if you aren't an overcommitter? You are probably a procrastinator. Like the overcommitter, procrastinators must ask themselves some questions too. Most obviously, do I really have a window in my schedule big enough to fit this task in tomorrow? And conversely, what keeps me from doing it now? Excuses can be silenced by adopting the watchword "just do it." Choosing to start something before you think it is necessary will begin to take you down a good path. This discipline will seem awkward at first. But the procrastinator will be rewarded by completed tasks and the dividend of personal pride.

These types of hurriers can also come in the disguise of optimists. Thinking there is plenty of time to get this little thing done later, they end up crammed and rushed at the last minute. They never think something is too daunting to fit in—tomorrow. Confident that it will only take a few minutes to do something, they see those "few minutes" begin to multiply exponentially into an insurmountable "to-do" list for tomorrow. This type of hurrier also needs to learn the reality of time-versus-task assessment. They don't commit to too many things like the overcommitter, but instead they inevitably underestimate the amount of time it will take to accomplish something. Both the overcommitter and the procrastinator can be caught wearing the "it will only take five minutes" rose-tinted glasses.

Procrastinators also tend to avoid uncomfortable tasks or unpleasant things. But the reality is that something that is just plain undesirable today will not magically change by tomorrow.

Often procrastinators ultimately lack confidence and sabotage their own success. Rather than just tackling something at full-speed now, the procrastinator who lacks confidence in their abilities chooses to "wait" rather than risk failure. Then task after task piles up until success is not even a possibility. They leave a littered path of incomplete projects behind them. The optimism and avoidance collide to produce a full-fledged hurrier. Coming to grips with doing their best and being content with that is a starting point for change. A young boy in the New Testament taught us that if we give God whatever is in our lunch box, he will make it be enough. Five thousand were fed with two loaves and five fishes because a boy gave what he had and trusted God to make up the difference.

If we don't adopt a wellness approach to how we handle our time, we will always be running to catch up with ourselves. And hurry is no friend to rest.

Rabbi Dr. Michael Samuel shares a story from the book *Springs in the Valley*. He recounts how a traveler was making a long journey in the jungles of Africa. He had hired men from a local tribe to help carry loads and direct him on the path. The first day they made tremendous progress and marched fast and far. The second day, the traveler got up and was prepared to continue this pace. But the tribesmen sat and rested, refusing to move. When asked why, they told the traveler they had gone too fast the first day, and now they must give their souls a chance to catch up with their bodies.

Has your body run off from your soul? Have you hurried until you can't keep up anymore? Slow down. Allow the hurry to leave you, and restore a sense of balance to the pace you are keeping. Passion for life does not always mean faster. Listen for the slow and steady beat of your heart. It neither rushes nor waits, but carefully and rhythmically moves to the speed of life.

P H Y S I C A L   R E S T

Ceasing from *Hurrying*

Feasting on *Slowing Down*

*"Time is a fixed income and, as with any income,
the real problem facing most of us is how to live
successfully within our daily allotment."*

MARGARET B. JOHNSTONE

*"Time is God's way of keeping everything
from happening at once."*

UNKNOWN

*"For everything there is a season, and a time
for every matter under heaven."*

ECCLESIASTES 3:1 RSV

The debut of the nanosecond in the 1980s gave us
one more tool for the measuring of time. It lasts one
billionth of a second. For a bit of context, it takes
only 500 million nanoseconds to snap your finger.

I had just begun to relax about the 86,400 seconds I had
lost, wasted, used, saved, taken, or spent in one day, and
now I have to consider how many millions of nanoseconds
I just used up by snapping my finger. Now there's some
kindling for the guilt fire.

Drowning in the disappearance of nanoseconds, how can we slow down? How can we find a spirituality of time, and then feast on it? Perhaps a slightly more macro look will help.

We know that in the beginning, God measured off time in the form of morning and night, and this was one day. From there he collected seven days to form what we now call a week. He created seasons that gather into a year, and then years that assemble lifetimes. What we can clearly see is the rhythmic structure of time and its cycles. That rhythm indicates a God of order.

And throughout Scripture, we see that God never hurried. Moses wasn't called by God until he was 40, and then he didn't begin fulfilling his most famous job description until he was 80. Even then, God was not in a hurry to accomplish his plans. Eighty-year-old Moses led the Israelites around the desert for another 40 years before they came into the Promised Land. And in all this time, God was about redeeming his creation.

The culmination of his plan of redemption through Christ didn't take place for thousands of years (and untold nanoseconds). And then Christ's act of sacrifice didn't come about for 33 years after his birth. God has his own timetable. Living our lives in a reference of time that doesn't surrender to God's reference means a life of anxiety and frustration.

I have not mastered this step of surrender. I find myself wanting to wrestle minutes from God's hands for my loved ones' lives and my own. A recognition that "our days belong to the Lord" silences the fear that disease, violence, or despair will steal them. We can be calmed by the quiet assurance that God is in charge of our days and can begin "spending" time with a new attitude.

Consider the instruction found in the prayer Jesus taught his disciples in Matthew chapter six. Once the issue of "thy kingdom come, thy will be done" is settled, we know who should be in control of our time. Jesus prays for our present, "Give us this day our daily bread," then for our past, "Forgive us our debts," and finally for our future, "Lead us not into temptation, but deliver us from evil" (verses 11-13 KJV). In the course of five verses, all of our time is spoken for. God is intimately concerned about our past, present, and future.

But in the generosity of God's grace, he knows that we will not easily rest in that. Later in the same chapter of Matthew, he urges us not to be anxious about adding anything to our lives and reminds us not to fret about sowing and gathering. And here is where anxiety over time and its purpose bumps hardest against a balanced spirituality of time. Most of our Day-Timers are full of tasks and appointments dedicated to sowing and gathering. Whether our concerns are about clothing, household goods, cars and the like, or power, self-esteem, and accomplishment, we rarely feast on the spirituality of time. More likely, we are busy stripping the fields of time before they have become ripe for the feasting.

Consider a small exercise. Take three highlighters and color-code your Day-Timer. Use pink to highlight the things you are doing to sow and gather. Then perhaps a blue to highlight the things you are doing to live "thy kingdom come." And finally, use yellow to highlight the things you have scheduled to help take you to sabbath rest. If you are at all like me, you will be largely monochromatic. And not in shades of blue or yellow.

I recognize this is a broad approach. But somewhere between this and scheduling by the nanosecond you can find a healthy spirituality of time. You will need to pray and listen for what is appropriate for your life. Consider focusing on overarching goals for the big seasons of life, then more specific ones for yearly seasons, holidays, and other time-measured traditions. This will be the framework from which to suspend a scaffolding of days. Days will have mornings, afternoons, and evenings to consider. Each of which mark out their own plot of time in the building of a day. And from there we progress down to hours, moments, and fleeting thoughts. Make no mistake, the time will pass. Whether it is spent or lost, wasted or used, will be up to your own intentional approach. One person's wasted moment can be another's sacred one. But everyone's day will have 24 hours, not a nanosecond more or less.

This year, the shadow of my parents' illnesses has greatly colored the way I look at time. I am seeing much more blue and yellow. For certain, I have more intimately considered the issues of death and eternity. But I have also begun to value moments more. I have discovered room in my seemingly packed day to sit in the car when I get to the gym for my swim, and finish talking on my cell phone with my parents. It has become a sacred routine for me. I call them as I pull out of my driveway and drive over to the gym, and instead of trying to rush through to goodbyes when I pull in the parking lot, I put the car in park and linger long-distance in the moment with my parents. I have discovered the pool to be exactly where I left it the day before, with no threat of escaping if I don't slide into it by a certain time. I still have time for a hot shower and six minutes in the sauna, even if I have to sacrifice some blow-drying and perhaps eyeliner. I have found that there truly is plenty of time for the really important things in life. And everything else will have to find its own nanosecond to fit in, or else be a task that is lost—instead of time that is lost.

When I am sick, I allow myself to cuddle up with the quilt my mother's mother made for me. I use it only for those special occasions because it is terribly fragile. But the love and care and time that went into each of the stitches in that quilt—the last quilt she ever made—seems to have healing properties that at least soothe my soul if not my ailing body. Every square in the quilt was selected from scrap fabric saved over time and was hand-cut to the appropriate shape and size. Then each piece was strategically connected to the next until the whole emerged from the parts. And even then, much more time went into hand-quilting the cover to the batting and the backing.

After many years of snuggle duty, washing, and drying, now this quilt is rather like a deflated balloon the day after a birthday party. Some of the stitches have let go their hold on each other. I have not hand-stitched anything in a long time. The sewing machine is just so much faster. There are no more quilts being produced in my family, but the sabbath rest still drips off the edges of this multicolored time capsule. It is a sacred relic from a simpler time.

If it could actually speak, I think it would tell me to put away the sewing machine from time to time and thread a needle. And it reminds me that feasting on the spirituality of time will feather the nest of my sabbath rest with goodness.

Physical Rest Stops

*Ceasing from hurrying, feasting
on slowing down.*

1. Make a time pie. Draw a circle and section it off into pie pieces that relate to how you spend your days. Which pieces should be smaller, which should be bigger? You are cutting and serving the pie. Which pieces do you want to eat?

2. Eliminate superfluous time eaters that steal your windows of rest.

3. Surrender to naps. Winston Churchill and Leonardo da Vinci were great nappers. It sounds like something that would slow down your day in a bad way, but adding a nap will actually make you more effective and more productive.

4. Wake up 15 minutes earlier than you normally would once a week for a month. At the end of that month, you will have created one more hour to your day to help you cease from hurrying.

5. Do some relational housecleaning. Do you have relationships with people who take but don't give? Do they respect only their schedule? Do they somehow trivialize your use of time? Are they high-maintenance, defensive, and possessive of you?

6. Do something to build patience. Sew, bake, do relaxation exercises, but make sure it's something that, if hurried, is ruined. Sit in the time. Allow yourself to surrender to the pace of growth.

Ceasing from
Overconsuming

Feasting on *Contentment*

> *"Most people seek after what they do not possess and are thus enslaved by the very things they want to acquire."*
>
> ANWAR EL-SADAT

> *"Materialism is organized emptiness of the spirit."*
>
> FRANZ WERFEL

*L*iving rooms, dens, great rooms, family rooms—whatever you call them, they must have end tables. Mine had two comfortable chairs, one not-so-comfortable (but screaming with character) chair, a very large oversized upholstered bench/coffee table/footstool, and the obligatory couch/divan/sofa. I had collected the perfect lamps for the room over the past few months, but there were no end tables to put them on. Instead, TV trays sat beside the chairs, serving as temporary tables—sort of like good "friends" going to the dance together instead of real "dates" who might actually kiss at the end of the evening.

I had no tables kissing my chairs. And I have just enough of the romantic in me that this would never do.

The problem is, I am rarely satisfied by a trip to the furniture store for my furniture needs. The many lean years that forced me to shop at salvage and thrift stores developed in me a quirky sense of style. I began to like the tossed off and unlikeable. I found fulfillment in recreating tired and unwanted pieces into redeemed items. In the context of my 1920s cottage, they became one-of-a-kinds instead of discarded trash. The writer in me cannot help but swoop on this lovely word picture of trash to treasure, redemption's old story unveiling itself in my own home. The woman of faith in me can't help but see the incarnation at work, rescuing the unloved and unwanted.

But aside from these lovely timeless truths revealing themselves, what about my tables?

I tried to reform the junk-store shopper in me, reminding myself I had more budget to work with now and could shop where big people shop for furniture. I combed the aisles of household-goods stores, and not once did an end table request the honor of my presence. The only pieces I was tempted by were simple architectural tables with paradoxically outrageous prices. It seemed that the simpler they came, the more they cost. So I drove myself again directly to one of my newly discovered antique stores.

I think I am romanced by the price and uniqueness, but perhaps even more by the out-of-the-way location, of my favorite stores. So I head to one located on a one-way street in a "don't go there after dark" neighborhood. But once inside, I encounter rows of individually rented booths filled with undiscovered treasures. Here, a delicate collection of English teacups and ladylike slipper chairs in one booth is juxtaposed with a collection of stovepipes, cement water trays, and various other architectural salvage pieces in the next booth. There, 1950s aprons and tablecloths spread out on diner-style tables and chairs sit next to what are now retro lamps from the 1980s. I wipe the drool from the edge of my mouth.

I feel certain that I hear my end tables calling to me from inside this former-train-station-become-antique-store. And after only a few moments of browsing the decades represented by all of these tchotchkes and castaways, I find my tables. A perfectly 29-inch tall rusted iron basket ($18) in one booth becomes the base for a 30-inch round piece of glass ($30) in another. Two aisles and several decades separate it from my second table. This time, a $45 jewel I will have to coax from its tired skin. A peeling, orangey oak table has the architecture and lines I flirted with in the big furniture store. I examine it for unrepairability—gashes and the like—and discover it is perfectly redeemable.

In the heat and humidity under the maple tree in my front yard, I sand every inch of the oak table down to pure nakedness. The pale white oak is smooth and imitates the skin of a woman in a Jane Austen novel. I stain it a dark coffee—espresso to bring it into a modern sensibility, and as I liberally paint on the stain with a foam brush, I am pleased by what I see. I leave the newly darkened table sitting on an old spotted and stained sheet until night, when I suppose it will be dry enough to carry inside to a temporary holding place.

Four hours later I am surprised at how wet it still is. I glove my hands and carefully carry it to its holding spot. Surely by morning it will be dry. It is not. Surely by the weekend it will be dry. It is not. Three months and two days later it is in my den, and you will want to be careful about brushing up against it, because it is still not dry.

The little table consumed all the stain it needed, and the rest sits in useless layers, potentially vicious, ready to mar people and objects. Sometimes, a good thing can be overdone.

In America, the land of the free, we enjoy an affluence unlike that of any other country in the world. Capitalism thrives in an economy that encourages the free operation of supply and demand. Unfortunately, the freedom to consume has produced overconsumers in almost every facet of life. There was a point in all of our lives when we had enough, but we continue to consume—to the point where it is not healthy. The stain of consumption sits in unhealthy layers on the skin of our culture, threatening to mar the quality of life we lead. Yes, sometimes a good thing can be overdone.

The American Dream drips with excess. More, bigger, newer, better. Everything is "biggie" sized. In 1996, *The Index of Social Health* indicated that while our per-capita consumption had risen by 45 percent since 1957, our quality of life had gone down by 52 percent. The statistics indicate that more does not necessarily equal happier.

The mall has now become our ultimate destination point. I heard someone remark once on how big $100 looks at church and how small it looks at the mall. To maintain our mall habit, we have to work increasing numbers of hours at jobs that are decreasingly fulfilling. Work begets money, money begets stuff, stuff begets temporary satisfaction. We are caught in a downward-spiraling cycle of craving, satisfaction, dissatisfaction, craving, satisfaction, dissatisfaction. To be sure, it always ends with dissatisfaction. The advertising industry seizes on our addiction to consuming and feeds the beast with products designed for obsolescence.

There is a term that describes our fallen state: *affluenza,* the disease of overconsumption. PBS did a special on affluenza in 1998 and described the symptoms of this ailment this way:

> "The bloated, sluggish and unfulfilled feeling that results from efforts to keep up with the Joneses."

- "An epidemic of stress, overwork, waste and indebtedness caused by dogged pursuit of the American Dream."

- "An unsustainable addiction to economic growth."

PBS also says that Americans have used more resources since 1950 than everyone who ever lived before then.

A three-car garage, not atypical with many homes today, is the size of the average home of the 1950s. American garages are full of the stuff we had to have that we don't use anymore. It is garage-filling season where I live right now. In my mailbox, mail-catalog season begins in earnest in October, and the opportunities to buy are endless. Web sites selling sausage-makers and skunk essence convince me our consuming is out of control. We had enough, a long time ago, but we keep piling it on.

We are trying to fill a void inside, but it was never designed to be filled this way. We trade quality of life for quantity of stuff. Our attempt to fill the emptiness with material things has resulted in existential disorders like chronic boredom, ennui, jadedness, purposelessness, meaninglessness, and alienation.

We are the walking wounded, but at least we have new shoes.

Sabbath rest invites us to cease from our consuming. I would not want you to hear me say that having things is wrong. But as my husband says repeatedly, "It's not wrong to have things, it's wrong for things to have you." So start small. Take a sabbath rest from the catalogs you get this week. Consider a mall "fast." Enforce delayed gratification this week, and don't buy anything nonessential until you go home and think about it for a day. Pull out some stuff stored in the garage and revisit it. Give something away instead of buying something. Practice consumer abstinence for a season. Recycle something bound for the trash.

And if you come across an extra table in your dumpster-diving, call me. I might be interested.

Ceasing from *Overconsuming*

Feasting on *Contentment*

"Christian contentment is that sweet, inward, quiet, gracious frame of spirit, which freely submits to and delights in God's wise and fatherly disposal in every condition."

JEREMIAH BURROUGHS

"And lovingly I pray to thee, O God, by your goodness give me yourself, for you are enough for me."

JULIAN OF NORWICH

"Now godliness with contentment is great gain."

1 TIMOTHY 6:6 NKJV

here were hot Krispy Kreme doughnuts on the table. There were also multi-flavors of pastry, bagels, and coffee cakes. It is not difficult for me to resist previously frozen packaged pastry, day-old coffee cake, or rock-hard bagels. But is it normal to reject a hot glazed doughnut? I say not.

I stood at the table, disguised as an adult woman in hose and heels, but inside I felt like a child with covert access to the cookie jar. Quiet hymns of faith were piped in through the ceiling while others of my gender—also in their disguises of heels and hose—accompanied by their males dressed up like men in sports coats and ties, casually passed along the "table of temptation." Some of them filled cups with the sacred fluid of caffeine, then turned the oil-black liquid sand-brown with sugar and milk. Most did not leave the table without selecting a doughnut, and some brazenly dunked right there in the fellowship hall. Only the pencil-thin women with the permanent smiles did not fall prey to the slithering-snake doughnuts.

The longer I stood there, the more convincing my thoughts became. At least I did not drink the evil coffee, which in itself could provide me with the excuse for possibly even two doughnuts. The fact that I had my red-and-white can of cola caffeine in my hand did not confuse the facts for me. (It was, after all, diet.) The most incriminating fact was that I wasn't hungry, having already eaten a sensible breakfast of turkey bacon and one egg. But hot doughnuts before Sunday school are almost an eleventh commandment. How could they be sinful if they were placed right here within my reach in the middle of church? How much was required of me on this Lord's Day morning?

That was the beginning of the day. From doughnuts chased with Diet Coke I moved on to pizza at lunch. By the afternoon I had a need for Cheetos and another Diet Coke, and then a bit later some of those little white-powdered doughnuts. When dinner came, I seized on the opportunity for tacos and chips with Diet Coke, and then finished off the day with a little bowl of cereal before bedtime. I continually said "yes" to each opportunity for food. At each feeding, I was responding to my body's screaming out for sustenance. But because I continued to try and satisfy the cravings with less-than-nutritious food, my body began a self-destructive relationship with counterfeit confections, and I went to bed bloated instead of full, fooled instead of satisfied.

When there is a hole in my stomach, sending in a load of empty calories will fill the hole only temporarily and ultimately will not nourish me. It also sets in motion an unhealthy craving for more of those empty sugary calories as my body goes in search for what it needs. When you don't get the nutrients you need, your body craves the foods that will provide the greatest and fastest stimulation. But eating foods low in nutritional value puts a stress on your system and eventually frustrates it.

In this same way, we frustrate our own attempts at contentment. Whether it is food or products, overconsuming has become the suburban addiction. It seems there is a hole in our souls that craves sustenance, and we continually feed it counterfeit confections instead of true soul satisfaction.

When we feel a longing in our souls, we tend to reach for what will provide the quickest satisfaction. The things we settle for are low in soul-nutrition value, and we fall into the same trap as we do with poor eating. And we wonder why we go to sleep night after night with an emptiness inside.

How can we tame the cravings and be freed from the addictions? What we are truly hungry for is contentment, and only this will bring the soul nourishment that we so desire. The writer of Ecclesiastes knew something about the vanity of temporary satisfactions. He wrote in chapter four, "Better a handful with quietness than both hands full, together with toil and grasping for the wind" (verse 6 NJKV). In other words, it is better to have less, as long as it is soul-nourishing, than to have abundance that is hollow.

The apostle Paul knew about contentment. He delivered his simple wisdom in the fourth chapter of his letter to the Philippians: "I have learned, in whatever state I am, to be content" (verse 11 RSV). This is a statement I long to be able to make.

Notice that he *learned* contentment. It isn't a state of being that you magically enter by meditation or special entitlement. No, it is a fruit produced only in the daily experience of life. Paul did not learn to be content because he lived in the most comfortable of circumstances. In fact, he spent more than a little time in prisons and confinement. His home was often a patch of dirt floor, and his outfits were sometimes accessorized with chains. If Paul learned to be content even in those times of his life, this tells us that contentment is not found in the things we can collect or the comfort of our surroundings.

Contentment is not just a mind game of convincing yourself that what you have is enough. That is a futile pursuit. Self-deception will only produce angry and frustrated people who ultimately resort to "bingeing" in some way or another. Recognizing that we have wants and desires is a part of the learning process. Putting words to our longings helps us to begin to examine the potential sources for satiating them.

Our ultimate wish list, unedited by money or circumstance, is a window into our soul. Sometimes a list like this helps us more accurately diagnose what it is we are trying to satisfy. What is it, we should ask ourselves, that we are spending all of our sabbath rest on? Will it really refresh us? A list of expensive cars and big houses may indicate a desire for status. Lists that are full of clothes and other appearance-oriented things may show our hunger for self-esteem or desirability. Job promotions, accolades, awards, or accomplishments hint at a desire for power. These things are not sinful in and of themselves, but they are not ultimate satisfiers or contentment-deliverers. Having nice cars, homes, and things, or being attractive or powerful, does not make you a bad person. But it likely has not made you a content person. The lesson learned in the daily experience of life is that if you are not enough without these things, then you will never be enough *with* them.

A.W. Pink said, "This much, then, is clear: contentment comes from within, not without; it must be sought from God, not in creature comforts." Contentment is a product of trusting that the God of all abundance knows my needs and will provide for my greatest good. God wants so much for us to know his generous provision that he did the same miracle twice in the New Testament. Two times he multiplied meager offerings to abundantly satisfy hungry people. Notice he did not tell them all to visualize full stomachs, and they would be full. He did not play mind games with the people, but generously supplied their needs.

The problem is, I don't always trust that he will provide. I think that someplace deep inside I am afraid that he wants me to suffer and go without. This is a deception that blocks my opportunity to be seized by a great affection. My fears can only be melted in the confident assurance that a loving God truly desires my highest good. And only as I choose this intimacy with God will he reveal himself to be the fullness of life in my soul.

As we choose this learning of contentment, there will be thieves who threaten to steal it from us at any moment. Practically speaking, I know of three thieves in particular.

Comparison is a contentment thief. Nancy McGuirk says that comparing yourself or what you have or don't have with other people will leave you feeling either smug or small. Neither of which is the fruit of contentment.

Living out of the moment will steal your contentment. Wanting to be somewhere or somewhen else will cause you to miss all of the possibilities in this moment. We are not called to "there"—we are called to "getting there." The journey, not the destination, is where we can find our contentment. We must learn to soak up all of the subtle satisfactions found in the sacred now.

An ungrateful heart is probably the most subversive of contentment thieves. Busily grumbling about what we don't have and using all of our time to pursue those things will leave us with bitter and hollow souls. In direct contrast, gratitude is the access door to contentment. If we are constantly being grateful for what we have, there will be no time or room for the entanglements of empty stuff.

Be aware of the contentment thieves as you choose to learn contentment. And perhaps we can say with our older brother Habakkuk, "Though the fig tree do not blossom, nor fruit be on the vines, the produce of the olive fail and the fields yield no food, the flock be cut off from the fold and there be no herd in the stalls, yet I will rejoice in the LORD, I will joy in the God of my salvation. GOD, the Lord, is my strength; he makes my feet like hinds' feet, he makes me tread upon my high places" (3:17-19 RSV). Contentment looks like walking in your high places. That doesn't sound meager or slight. It sounds like *enough*.

Physical Rest Stops
Ceasing from overconsuming, feasting
on contentment.

1. Make a gratitude list. Thank God for one thing on that list each day. Notice that your list grows. Gratitude begets gratitude. It is hard to find room for new possessions when you are feasting on the ones you have.

2. Frame something that is in your closet. Either take a photo and have it blown up at your copy store, or rescue one of the children's drawings, or pull out a map of someplace you have gone for a vacation. Find something new in something old.

3. When a craving to shop comes over you, use it. Instead of shopping for yet "more stuff" for yourself, enjoy shopping and accomplishing something at the same time. Take a birthday shopping trip. Decide on a theme for the year and shop for the people you buy birthday presents for. For example, I selected slippers as a theme once. I had a plan when I went out, and I enjoyed shopping for unique slippers. When I gave them to everyone, I welcomed them to the "Ya-Ya Slipperhood." This can satisfy the desire to shop and the need to purchase birthday presents without adding to your "consuming" habit.

4. Take a "theme walk." Decide how long you will walk, and then pick something to mentally dwell on that will build contentment. "Theme" possibilities:

- Go through the alphabet and think of something to be grateful for with each letter.

⌒ Consider trees and how uniquely they are made, rejoicing that our heavenly Father created them for our enjoyment. Look at each tree you pass with a new sense of thankfulness.

⌒ Fill up on the vastness of the sky. Breathe deeply and quietly sing the doxology.

When you get home, you will have a quiet sense of contentment and rest.

Ceasing from *Crowds*

Feasting on *Solitude*

"Solitude is a necessary protest to the incursions and the false alarms of society's hysteria, a period of cure and recovery."

ABRAHAM HESCHEL

"He withdrew himself into the wilderness, and prayed."

LUKE 5:16 KJV

"I love people. I love my family, my children…but inside myself is a place where I live all alone and that's where you renew your springs that never dry up."

PEARL S. BUCK

The sanguine personality thrives on conversation and being with people. It is in the middle of a luxuriant crowd of people that the sanguine person is refreshed and energized. The stimulation of conversation and company enlivens these souls. Those of us who tend more toward the melancholic personality find that time alone or in the company of one or two others is the fuel of life. Our family contains one of each. Jim befriends anyone he comes in contact with. I am the person on the airplane who wears her earplugs and eye-blinders, giving off the "not available for interaction" signal.

But even the sanguine eventually needs time away from the crowds. Noise, interaction, and the assault of other lives can cumulatively drain us until nothing more than the container is left of our souls. Sometimes we have wearied ourselves with crowds because we have simply been in pursuit of filling the emptiness we feel inside. This is a natural reaction, but trying to fill the void within us with finite stimulation, when its designed for the infinite, will leave us unsatisfied. In constant search of filling up, we give ourselves to crowds and gatherings, congregations and audiences, family and committees, and yet we still feel isolated and alienated. Proximity to other people will not satisfy our longing. It isn't harmful by nature to spend time in crowds, but again, with no pause the cumulative effect will steal our rest.

I'm not suggesting we enter a passive–aggressive state of calling people to ourselves and then pushing them away. We need a healthy balance of community and solitude. It is in fact the experience of bumping up against others that helps us define who we are, and who we aren't. And certainly we are called to nurture and encounter those around us. But even Christ took time to "come away" from the crowds.

Early in his life, before he began his ministry in full, Jesus went away from the crowds to a silent wilderness for 40 days. It was in this wilderness that the voices in his life were so clearly distinguished, and the foundation of truth was identified and spoken by his own lips. Coming away from the crowds is not just a self-indulgent opportunity for "self." The emptiness of solitude is transformed to something full and valuable when we cease from crowds in order to feed our starving souls.

Mammals solve the problem of scarcity of food in the winter with their own version of ceasing from crowds. They hibernate. They cloister themselves away in a quiet and warm place and slowly lower their metabolism. Outside of their den, they have little need, and they live on accumulated fat. During hibernation, the ground squirrel drops its respirations from 200 to 4 or 5 per minute, and its heart rate from 150 to 5 beats per minute. Its body slows down and pulls away from life to rest for a season. When the spring comes, signaling its biology to wake up, it emerges refreshed and ready for interaction with the world again.

Perhaps our spirits need to hibernate for seasons. When sensory overload threatens our reserves, we must consider this concept of cloistering. It may be hard for some personalities to even recognize the symptoms of too much input. For others of us, standing on a crowded subway train or elevator can spend us, sending screaming signals for crowd-ceasing into our ears. But either type of person will show signs of listlessness or edginess, low creative resources, and a general sense of fatigue when it is time to come away. Physical symptoms of headache and backache are common warning signals.

Consider this scenario. You left home early this morning, all seats in your minivan taken. You dropped the children off at school and went to work. Morning meetings preceded lunch with friends. The afternoon sent you to the mall and grocery store for necessities, and then the children had soccer, ballet, Scouts, and other important appointments. You come home and the TV is on, you have messages to listen to and e-mails to read, not to mention postal mail. You prepare dinner, help with three types of homework, return phone calls, and decompress the day with your husband. After tucking everyone in bed, watching some late-night television, and reading two paragraphs in your book, you turn off the light and lie back in the dark and silent bed. Your ears are ringing, and images print themselves on the inside of your eyelids. You are overtired, overspent, and in desperate need of hibernation.

Withdrawal and recollection are not only luxuries of the monastic community. They are necessities for the healthy survival of "you." You wouldn't think of draining your checking account and continuing to spend from it. If you do not intentionally cease from the crowds and come away, you may slip into the walking unconsciousness of the over-spent.

Crowds can be energizing and entertaining for a period, but we were designed to occasionally cease from the crowds and enter the rest of solitude. If that sounds like a good idea, then why not do it now?

Ceasing from *Crowds*
Feasting on *Solitude*

*"Language has created the word 'loneliness' to express
the pain of being alone, and the word 'solitude'
to express the glory of being alone."*

PAUL TILLICH

*"I never close my door behind me without the awareness
that I am carrying out an act of mercy toward myself."*

PETER HOEG

*"For it is God who makes solitude,
deserts and silences holy."*

CATHERINE DE HUECK DOHERTY

*I*t is in solitude when we learn that the pause from
doing ripens *being*.

In the fullness of the apple tree, the ripening
process begins in the solitude of each individual fruit.
Before ripening, the hard green flesh is sour, mealy, and has
no scent. But at a designated time, the fruit releases a burst
of ethylene gas, which stimulates the ripening process.
Sometimes it is a wound or an infection of bacteria that pro-
vokes that process. In any case, enzymes are produced to

help the starch in the fruit become sugar, and pectinase is released, which works on the texture of the fruit, softening up the hard flesh. Chlorophyll is broken down, and pigments are produced to change the skin from green to red, the exterior sign of an interior change. Enzymes also break down molecules that evaporate into the air and give off the resulting aroma, signaling to those within smelling distance that the apple is ripe. In this short season of pause, the fruit ripens.

When my days have no pause for solitude, when I am always "with" others, my heart can become hard, my exterior won't display evidence of a well-maintained spiritual interior, and I know I do not give off the scent of Christ wherever I go. I need a pause for ripening. In the sanctuary of solitude, my inner resources can be recharged and redirected toward connecting with God. It is a time of restoring spiritual equilibrium.

Solitude is the twin sister of silence. One can experience silence without solitude, but one cannot experience solitude without silence. While silence is about quiet, solitude adds the dimension of away-ness. As we take time to withdraw from people, the concentration of spiritual awareness can be amplified in silent solitude.

You can build an attitude of solitude in the midst of people, but the most rest-producing solitude is what we experience when we cease from crowds and come away. Even Christ took times to withdraw from the crowds so he might reconnect with the Father through times of prayer. His time in the desert, in preparation for his ministry, was truly a time of spiritual ripening as he affirmed and reaffirmed the truths of God. And at later times, after he and the disciples had been ministering to crowds, the Gospels tell us that he took time to withdraw and pray.

But it isn't enough just to come away. This is not just about "me" time. For the feast of solitude to become the ripening process of being, we will need to immerse ourselves in the presence of God. There is a common misconception that solitude is simply about emptying ourselves, or that it is about isolation and alienation. Nothing could be further from the truth. Solitude is not a time of emptiness—it is a time of fullness. It is a fullness that does not disappoint, a filling that overflows with contentment and refreshment. Solitude transforms isolation with the realization that we are never alienated and alone if we are believers walking in faith. Solitude is a concentrated time of quiet withdrawal when we peel back the curtain of alone, and we find the loving heavenly Father who delights in our being in his presence.

Challenge your schedule to find space for communing with God on an intimate level. Find a way to be "away." A walk in the woods, or on the beach, or up a mountain, gives us an opportunity to connect with God in a non-striving and easy manner. Dwell on how his generously creative hand has made each leaf unique, like a fingerprint. Or work in your garden and meditate on the promises of Scripture. Rhythmically swim laps and contemplate the attributes of God—his holiness, justice, faithfulness, and gentleness. Lie in a hammock and spill out quiet praises along with the invitation for the Holy Spirit to inhabit them, as the Psalms teach us. Sit on the floor of your shower with the water turned on hot and let the enveloping fog of solitude help you sit in the presence of God.

The "desert fathers" of our faith knew what it meant to feast on solitude. Many of these early men of faith felt a need to withdraw for the pursuit of quiet stillness. They used solitude as a way to deepen their prayer life. They discovered that the need for ongoing guidance of the spirit could best be found in times of coming away. There is a term that is used for this ancient tradition of coming away—the Greek word *hesychia*. Literally translated, this word means "the way of stillness, tranquility, or rest." Henri Nouwen says that a *hesychast* is someone who seeks solitude and silence as the ways to prayer. And the New Testament reminds us that rest and peace flow from prayer.

Do you long for a season of solitude, a season of ripening? Is your spirit in need of a time to reconnect with God on levels deeper than just sentence prayers? Have you given yourself away to the multitudes, and do you need a time of restoring?

The ripening process eventually affects a layer of cells near the stem of the fruit, where it is attached to the tree. Those cells ripen and thin until eventually the fruit drops, an animal picks it up, and the seeds are dispersed. Our time of solitude will allow us as well to ripen and fall to the ground, dispersing seeds of faith once again among the crowds.

Physical Rest Stops

Ceasing from crowds, feasting on solitude.

1. Choose to have lunch alone. Sit in a crowded restaurant and still be "away," or pick up a sandwich and eat under a quiet tree. Find a children's park and sip one of those "meal" shakes while you are on a swing. Drive somewhere you enjoy the view and eat in your car. Enjoy the provision for your body, but also drink in the solitude.

2. Take one hour for personal time. Find an old cathedral or country church that has historic character and sit in a pew. Listen to the quiet. Consider the faithful who have communed with God in that place over the years. Feel your spiritual connection to the body of Christ during that hour away.

3. Find a private corner in your public library. We have recently discovered our new downtown library. The high ceilings and vast number of rooms give ample choices of places to "come away." Libraries naturally have a spirit of solitude and quiet that will help you enter into rest.

4. Set up a reading time in your household. Everyone must have a "place" they go to for that time. It can be a chair, a room, the attic, the porch, or up in a tree. But the rule is, you must read, and must do it alone. You can all read the same book and plan to discuss it at Saturday-morning breakfast.

5. Sit by the stillness of water. It can be a pond, a lake, the ocean, or just a birdbath. Consider the reflections you see. Notice that the stiller the water, the clearer the reflections. Allow your heart to be stilled in that time of solitude so it can more accurately reflect the image of Christ as you leave that place.

6. Make a standing date with a cup of tea in the afternoons. Surrender your time so you can come away for the time it takes to have just one cup of tea—at a favorite restaurant, at your kitchen table, on your couch, in your car, or in your closet.

Be physical sabbath rest for someone else.

"The Sabbath is the inspirer, the other days the inspired."
ABRAHAM HESCHEL

Are you always so hurried and overcommitted that those around you lose their rest? Consider facilitating one of the "physical rest stop" ideas for someone you know who needs rest. Or take your sense of solitude with you so that someone you come into contact with might experience solitude for a moment.

Consider something you are in charge of. How can you reduce the "busyness" for the others involved? Buy some flowers and enjoy them for a day or two, and then, when there are still a few days of life left in them, give them away and share the gift. Make up a traveling tea set that you can take to a friend's house—and make them a cup of tea, sit in the quiet with them, and commit to leaving after one cup or one pot of tea.

Spiritual Rest

"The fruit of the Spirit is not push, drive, climb, grasp, and trample. Don't let the rat-racing world keep you on its treadmill. There is a legitimate place for blood, sweat, and tears; but it should have its roots in the call of God, not in the desire to get ahead. Life is more than a climb to the top of the heap."

RICHARD FOSTER

Ceasing from *Fear*

Feasting on *Trust*

"The most often repeated command in the Scripture is 'Do not fear.'"

K.T.

"We can easily forgive a child who is afraid of the dark; the real tragedy of life is when adults are afraid of the light."

PLATO

After my swim today, I lay back in the pool and let my arms go out at my sides. I pulled in a lot of air, and my body floated on the top of the water. Through my tinted goggles, I stared up at the ceiling 20 feet above my head. Just in view from the corner of my eye, red, green, yellow, and blue flags hung contentedly in the sun. Children and grown-ups continued playing in the water as if I wasn't there. I was happy to be invisible. I still had my earplugs in, so the screams of the children being entertained by the wonder that is a pool were just muffled voices far from my world. I lay there for as long as I could, on the edge between water and air. For just a few minutes I wanted to feel light again, not heavy from the gravity of fear that pulled me down. My compass bearing seemed to be just this side of heaven.

On September 11, 2001, my husband Jim and I spent the morning in fear, afraid that we had lost his mother in the attack on the Pentagon. She had worked there for close to a dozen years and was due to retire at the end of that month. That morning, she was in the section next to where the attack occurred and by God's mercy escaped unhurt. She and her colleagues from the Department of the Army Public Affairs Office got out of the building and were herded together to a metro subway stop about two miles down from the Pentagon. From there, she phoned Jim's brother who lives in the Washington, DC, area, and he in turn called us to tell us, "She got out."

We sat on our bed watching the horror of the morning, as did so many others, and we held our breath, afraid to let go of the air in our lungs because something might happen to keep us from getting more. I don't know anyone who didn't feel fear that day. In the face of mortality, the paper-thin wall between life and death doesn't feel strong enough to lean against.

When we were finally sure that Jim's mom was safe, we let out our breath and gulped in new air like starving beggars. By dinner, though, we were holding our breath again, this time about *my* mother.

She had been fighting bronchitis for too long, and the doctors were running tests to find out if there was more to the mystery. She was diagnosed that day with pulmonary fibrosis. My family was instantly frightened because someone else close to us had been diagnosed with pulmonary fibrosis and had been given a very bleak prognosis. After studying everything we could find on-line, we were mildly encouraged to learn that hers was one of the "better" kinds of pulmonary fibrosis (if there could be such a thing)—a secondary condition from "sarcoidosis." The lining of her lungs was being scarred over like concrete and her oxygen efficiency was being compromised.

In the next few weeks I began what would be more than a yearlong struggle with intense fear as I faced my parents' mortality. Six months into treating Mom, the doctors were evasive and less than confident about giving us a clear prognosis. She wasn't feeling any better, so my sister and I researched alternatives for her care and treatment. We had finally made a tentative appointment for her to come see a doctor here in Nashville at Vanderbilt University Hospital. But on Tuesday, the week before, Dad went to the doctor because his bronchitis had hung on for too long. This sounded all too familiar, and I found myself holding my breath again. Mom and Dad got the results of his tests and called to say they were trying to set up a conference call with both me and my sister—for just after four that afternoon, two hours away.

Fear is measurable, conspicuous, and heavy. I felt the adrenaline rush through my body as my "fight or flight" response hijacked reason and logic. I knew the news must be sober if a conference call was necessary. I took my body and all of its surging fear for a walk around the cul-de-sac we live on. I breathed shallow breaths of whispered prayer. "O God, please. O God, please. O God, please." The third time around the cul-de-sac I sat down on the curb four houses down from ours. I was subconsciously looking through the clover patch and found a four-leaf clover. I've always been good at finding them. Today I was glad. I pulled the little anomaly from the earth and twirled it between my fingers. Two of the leaves were perfect, two of them were slightly mangled, not exactly right. There is no theology for this, only the existential reality of Presence. I was at peace with the fact that everything was going to be okay. Things wouldn't be exactly right, but they would be okay.

The four o'clock phone call revealed that my dad had lung cancer. Fear of the unknown suddenly ripened in full within my already bruised soul, and I pictured the two mangled leaves of my clover. Mom and Dad were sick.

All the plans for Mom to come here were put on hold as my sister and I helped them research the best place for Dad to be treated. Time went by in slow motion and fast forward all at the same time. Voices seemed muffled, and food even tasted different, with my adrenal glands influencing all of my senses. We settled on a doctor in Houston for Dad's treatment, which was good because my sister lived there. I was so grateful it was her, my big sister, and not me, because I was lost to my fears and of little help to anyone else. She graciously and willingly rose to the challenge. I loved from afar and got free long distance for my cell phone.

◦◦◦

Fear takes you on a ride from quiet apprehension to loud agitation. I found that mornings were the hardest for me. The pause of a night's sleep would restore my senses just enough for me to be aware of the new reality all over again. And the fear of being a child without parents sat on me with no indication of leaving. Where fear does not take you is to rest. There were no sabbath pauses, no rests of refreshment, no deep breaths of certainty.

The following weeks would take us from four doctors saying "yes, lung cancer," to new doctors saying "no, it's lymphoma," to yet more new doctors saying "no, it's a blocked carotid artery." My vocabulary blossomed in areas I never wanted it to as I researched each new diagnosis on the computer. Finally, after surgery, the thoracic surgeon came out to tell us it wasn't any of those things—it was a fungal infection and, though it was serious, it was not life-threatening. We exhaled fear and inhaled life. Glorias fell from our lips, alleluias trailing them.

While Dad was being treated, my sister set up appointments for Mom. The appointments eventually confirmed her diagnosis, and it was decided that, while her condition was life-altering, it too was not life-threatening.

The next two months were a pause to collect ourselves and gather stamina. It had been one year and one month since the initial diagnosis that had invited fear into our lives. Now, fear dissolved into quiet resolve as Mom and Dad went home to Orlando after three months in Houston. Mom was set up with doctors there whom we all felt a level of confidence in, and things began to feel right again. We all made plans for going "home" for Christmas—anything to make it feel like it used to when things were normal. Before all the sickness. Before all the fear made a nest in my soul. Christmas at Mom and Dad's house would make things like they used to be.

Scripture reminds us that life is but a vapor. It passes quickly, like a communion wafer that sits on my tongue—present to me, and then gone. Mom and Dad went to Houston for Thanksgiving, for follow-up tests. Dad showed distinct improvement, and Mom was looking better. They did, however, find that a mass in her lung had grown since the last visit, and they felt compelled to do a biopsy. None of us were extremely concerned—after all, she had a lung disease, so there were probably things in there that shouldn't be, but nothing frightening.

Yesterday we found out it is indeed lung cancer. Next week we start all over again with tests and then procedures, prognosis, and prescription. Christmas plans are on hold now—they will probably be moved to Houston and hospitals. That will become home because Mom and Dad will be there.

I would walk the cul-de-sac, but it is winter now, and all the clover patches are gone. Maybe the cold wind would be good, forcing me to stop holding my breath, making me breathe in and out. But fear reduces me to alternating states of tears and stoic resignation, and I'm not in the mood for walking. I am tired. I must trade fear for rest. I will breathe in and out only because I am certain God knows my name and calls me his own. Isaiah 43 tells me so. He promised that when the waters get high, he'll be with me. The water is high—I can only throw my arms out and float, somewhere between here and heaven, buoyed by his presence.

Ceasing from *Fear*
Feasting on *Trust*

"Thou wilt keep him in perfect peace, whose mind is
stayed on thee: because he trusteth in thee. Trust ye
in the LORD for ever: for in the LORD JEHOVAH
is everlasting strength..."

ISAIAH 26:3-4 KJV

If we do not believe the theology of our faith, there is no reason to trust. If there is no reason to trust, there is no rest.

Without a reliable theology, there is no reason for my family and me to survive the grief of illness, mortality, and separation. If the object of my trust is not trustworthy, I might as well surrender to my fears and draw the curtains of life around me. If I am not simply thrown down at the feet of a merciful God in whom are all things, all of my frail attempts at entering sabbath rest will be insincere and temporary at best.

Trust is the firm reliance on the integrity of God. It is the assurance that our faith-expectations are founded in truth. I could be creative and give you "Five Steps to Rest When You Are Fearful," but every one of them would be temporary pauses in seasons of fear. If we are not first grounded in who God is and what we can count on in the theology of our faith, we will live our life in search of temporary Band-Aids for our wounded souls.

⌒ · ⌒ · ⌒

I am not the theologian in our family. That is Jim's job. I am the one who takes pleasure in stories and contemplative approaches to life. But when I am in a season of fear that snuggles up next to doubt, it is only theology that will sustain me. Jim has said that the church has been guilty of teaching therapy instead of theology. As teachers, many of us have tried to put people at ease in their skin, and have tried to give solutions to the stress and struggles of daily life. But all of the practical and therapeutic steps on how to live a more fulfilling life will fail us at some point. No matter how many times we check our "to-do" lists, life will inevitably mess up our well-crafted plans and throw us, ultimately, on the mercy of what can only be a sustaining faith. So, being that I am at least in close proximity to a true theologian, may I remind us of some of the reasons that our faith is reliable and therefore trustworthy?

Everything I have said in this book is important only if we recognize first that the reason we cease from our labors is because the "work" has been completed. That is, the work of our salvation has been completed in the life, death, and resurrection of Christ Jesus. Christ came to earth and was not murdered, but offered his life as a sacrifice, completing the work of redemption planned since the beginning of time. He defeated sin and death in his sojourn on the cross, and rest became a reality for the believer.

Hebrews 4:9 tells us that there is a rest for the people of God. Heaven is our ultimate place of redeemed rest. It is the promise to the believer that at the end of this journey of flesh and blood, there is a rest that does not disappoint. But the spiritual rest that we can enter into now—that we

150

don't have to wait for heaven to experience—is the confidence that the work required to secure our salvation is done. No efforts or labors will purchase what has been given freely. The only labor required is to believe. This is the theology that undergirds the effectiveness of any therapy or "how-to's" in our pursuit of rest. Remember that God did not rest in Genesis chapter 2 because he was exhausted. He rested because his work was done. God has labored to redeem us, the labor was complete in Christ, and so we rest in that.

"I believe in God the Father almighty, maker of heaven and earth." If we believe this first sentence of the Apostle's Creed, one of the most basic assertions of the Christian faith, then we have truly begun to feast on trust. The all-encompassing transcendent mystery of "almighty" and the personal, knowable, and immanent "Father"—this is the Maker of all things. It is he who holds my days. I am not at the mercy of a world gone out of control. My mother is not subject to the whim of the cancer cells in rebellion in her body. We do not live and die, or exist day to day, at the hands of a random expression of quantum physics. Because I believe in God the Father, I also believe in the "forgiveness of sins, the resurrection of the body, and life everlasting"; that is, the rest of now, and the rest of heaven.

This reliable, rock-solid theology gives me reason to rest on a daily basis in the "now" that is my life. If I merely had the hope of heaven, salvation and its promise would be nothing but a tease, the promise of a future with no hope for today. But the hope of heaven is spirited into each moment in the form of the peace I find when trusting in the Lord. He is trustworthy, and the works he does through whatever he chooses in my life are often beyond my understanding. But he doesn't abandon me to unrest. As I make my fears known to God, the peace he promises in Philippians chapter four will transcend all of my understanding, and it will guard my heart and mind.

I may not always understand, but I can rest. As Rilke says, we must live the questions until one day we wake up to see that we have lived into the answers. Putting away fear and feasting on trust, we rest in the reliability of God. He promises that the things we endure that cause fear and anxiety will eventually develop character in us that will make us complete, lacking in nothing (James 1:2-3). I may not always trust that circumstances will work out for my happiness, but I can rest confidently in the fact that they will result in God's highest good for me.

I e-mailed my friend to tell her about my mother's newly diagnosed cancer. Days of silence from her ended today with a return e-mail. Maggie's dad had had a stroke and was declining quickly. She was on her way to be with him. I was startled over our parallel lives, and was strangely comforted by our common sufferings. Second Corinthians 1 tells us that it is these sufferings that lead us to the comfort of Christ, with which we comfort one another.

Maggie told me she was dwelling on a verse for this advent season from Habakkuk chapter one, which says that we are to watch and be amazed at the wonders that will be done in our days, things that will baffle our minds. She suggested that perhaps this was the season she and I were in. So I plant my feet in the clay of this earth and prepare to be amazed—as God, the reliable and trustworthy Almighty and Father, leads me from the unrest of fear to the rest of trust.

Spiritual Rest Stops
Ceasing from fear, feasting on trust.

1. Make a list of your worst fears. Take one each day and pray for God to deliver you from the fear that steals your rest. Dwell on these verses:

- ◯ Psalm 3:6: "I will not fear the tens of thousands drawn up against me on every side."

- ◯ Psalm 23:4: "Even though I walk through the valley of the shadow of death, I will fear no evil, for you are with me; your rod and your staff, they comfort me."

- ◯ Psalm 33:18: "The eyes of the LORD are on those who fear him, on those whose hope is in his unfailing love."

- ◯ Psalm 34:7: "The angel of the LORD encamps around those who fear him, and he delivers them."

- ◯ Proverbs 19:23: "The fear of the LORD leads to life: then one rests content, untouched by trouble."

- ◯ Proverbs 29:25: "Fear of man will prove to be a snare, but whoever trusts in the LORD is kept safe."

- ◯ Isaiah 41:10: "Do not fear, for I am with you; do not be dismayed, for I am your God. I will strengthen you and help you; I will uphold you with my righteous right hand."

- ◯ Isaiah 41:13: "For I am the LORD, your God, who takes hold of your right hand and says to you, Do not fear; I will help you."

○ Isaiah 43:1-2: "This is what the Lord says—he who created you, O Jacob, he who formed you, O Israel: 'Fear not, for I have redeemed you; I have summoned you by name; you are mine. When you pass through the waters, I will be with you; and when you pass through the rivers, they will not sweep over you. When you walk through the fire, you will not be burned; the flames will not set you ablaze.'"

○ Haggai 2:5: "This is what I covenanted with you when you came out of Egypt. And my Spirit remains among you. Do not fear."

○ Matthew 10:28: "Do not be afraid of those who kill the body but cannot kill the soul. Rather, be afraid of the One who can destroy both soul and body in hell."

○ Romans 8:15: "You did not receive a spirit that makes you a slave again to fear, but you received the Spirit of sonship. And by him we cry, '*Abba*, Father.'"

○ 1 Peter 3:14-15: "Even if you should suffer for what is right, you are blessed. 'Do not fear what they fear; do not be frightened.' But in your hearts set apart Christ as Lord."

○ 1 John 4:18: "There is no fear in love. But perfect love drives out fear, because fear has to do with punishment. The one who fears is not made perfect in love."

(All of the above verses are from the NIV.)

2. Beware of weeds. Thomas Merton says that every event and every moment plants something in our souls. There is a weed called the bearded darnel that looks identical to wheat when the two are growing together. Be alert, fear is a bearded darnel. It disguises itself as caution, but it is fear. When the bearded darnel is fully grown, it can be distinguished from the mature wheat by one characteristic. The fruit of the wheat causes it to bow low. The bearded darnel stands stiff-necked. When fear takes root in our lives and matures, we are not bowing to the trustworthiness of God. The fruit of the Spirit growing in our lives will cause us to bow. We must do some weeding.

3. Grow healthy fruit. Allow the Spirit to plant and nurture his fruit in your life. Love, joy, peace, patience, kindness, goodness, faithfulness, gentleness, self-control. Eventually, these plants will naturalize in the garden of your heart and grow more easily.

4. Purchase a cup. Call it the "thy will be done" cup. In Luke 22:42, Jesus prayed this about what he feared: "Father, if you are willing, take this cup from me; yet not my will, but yours be done" (NIV). Write your fears on pieces of paper and put them in the cup. It is not wrong to have fears, but we should give them to the Lord. If we begin to seek his will over ours, the fears become secondary to building his kingdom.

Ceasing from
Hard-heartedness

Feasting on *the Prayer of Examen*

*"The most dangerous thing is that the soul, by the neglect
of little things, becomes accustomed to unfaithfulness."*

FRANÇOIS FENELON

"I must be ploughed up and resown."

C.S. LEWIS

andinas are friendly bushes that need little or
no tending. These are my favorite specimens of
horticulture. They require no fussy trimming,
they don't need staking up when their heads get heavy,
and they aren't susceptible to every fungus or rude insect.
They simply do their job of greening up in the spring and
summer, changing color to a deep green and red in the
fall, and berry-ing in the winter. They are no threat to
neighboring plants, and their root systems are not
demanding.

I have five nandinas. That is not counting the dwarf nandinas that sit in a semicircle in a front bed. The purchase
price on these bushes indicated their "shrub of the people"
identity. When I bought them in five-gallon buckets for
under $10 each, they were even a respectable size (unlike
certain other bushes that sit in five-gallon buckets but are

really just sticks that belong in one-gallon buckets). We had recently purchased our beloved 1920s cottage, which was delightfully naked in the landscaping category, and the generous-looking nandinas were choice picks. The sparse landscaping suited me fine because, frankly, I preferred to plant what I wanted rather than to have to spend time digging up unsatisfactory shrubbage. We dug small holes—not nearly the size recommended by the nursery—and stuffed the little nandina root balls in them. We didn't fertilize. We didn't water. No thanks to us, they flourished, and rewarded us with graceful branches full of pointed leaves that bounced in the slightest wind.

One Nashville winter, we were hit with a very hard ice storm. In all of the 15 years I've lived here, that is the worst one I remember. We were traveling a good bit that year and only experienced the lingering effects ourselves, but the stalwart nandinas took a full frontal assault. By the time the ice melted, the top third of the bushes had succumbed to the weight and thickness of the ice. Their long and graceful branches were randomly snapped off as well, and all in all, our front landscaping bed looked a little like the smile of a seven-year-old child. Some teeth completely missing and others in various stages of "grown in."

I felt the pressure of suburbia and decided the nandinas were not up to front-yard appearance. We dug small holes in the side yard and transplanted them.

They have been roving ever since.

When we built the fence, they had to get out of the way of the postholes, and so they were transplanted to the back of the house. They only suffered a little in that move, and then they proceeded to truly thrive. Every time I would get a glance of them from the back alley, I would mentally thrash myself for not having believed in them enough to give them a second front-yard chance. This past year, we did some construction on the house, and they were once again in the way. So a very big man driving a very big backhoe dug them up, not very carefully, and deposited them in a rear corner of our yard. The winter was coming much too soon, and all we could do for the nandinas was just shovel some loose soil over their exposed roots. This spring they stood at attention, not quite in peak form, but ready for their next assignment.

My ultimate plan for them had been a home in a distinctly bare place in the backyard that bordered my perennial garden and fence. I sketched them all in position and settled the decision. I waited for a not-too-hot but not-too-cold spring afternoon and put my garden spade to the task. I jumped on the spade to force it down into the sleeping soil...and disturbed only a slight furrow. I reared back and really jumped on it this time, thinking that a long winter's nap was holding the soil tightly in place. Again my spade barely poked its fingernails into the ground. I determined that I would need more brute force than my 145 pounds (okay, 148) could deliver. I called for Jim to stop whatever he was doing and come assist me in the transplant effort. He loves to help me by doing the labor-intensive parts of any chore, so he put his gardening shoes on and innocently shoved the spade dirtward. Three more attempts, and he was not much further along than my little ditch attempt. We decided that the firmness of the ground demanded larger tools.

Many weeks later, our contractor brought the most adorable piece of equipment to our house to begin to push around the piles of dirt from the year's construction. He barely wedged his large frame into the control seat of the Bobcat and began scooting around the backyard. We directed him to the prescribed area to dig up a long bed for the nandinas, and he confidently rolled the tanklike unit over there. Repeated attempts with this high-powered digger failed.

The soil in that section of the yard was hard as cement. It seems that even the topsoil had abandoned the area, leaving only a slight head of grass to survive there. The soil would need reconstituting if it is ever going to be able to receive new plants and produce lush growth.

And the nandinas continue to have no permanent home. They sit in garden purgatory, awaiting a fertile bed of earth.

⁓ · ⌒ · ⌒

I have a heart composed of various soil types. I even give off the illusion of spiritual fertility, but in many ways I carry a hard heart that resists new plantings.

Sabbath rest invites me to cease my hard-heartedness. But I carry my thoughts and emotions tied in a tight little ball that safely protects the deeper places of me. I resist the urging of the Spirit to trust that God will care for me, and instead I bundle myself under layers of resistance that, after years of pressure, become rock.

A hard heart resists new ways. It stands by its old ways (regardless of how rarely they succeed) because stubborn is sometimes safer than vulnerable. A hard heart doesn't adjust in the midst of change. It panics and puts up walls of immovability. It is not flexible in the fluidness of uncertainty. It neglects the daily fidelities in search of more glamorous trimmings. A hard heart is not generous with its resources because they have become slight. It doesn't risk, receive, or blossom. It sits in an unpliable state of isolation.

Sabbath rest calls us to softened hearts. God speaks to Ezekiel and promises to turn hearts of stone to hearts of flesh.

I want a heart that is open to new plantings. I don't want to be so tightly wound that there is ultimately no access to me. I've learned that I need to consciously instruct myself to let go and trust. When I do that, I can actually feel the muscles in my stomach unclench. My shoulders drop to a relaxed position, and my breathing deepens. I am ready for sabbath rest.

Ceasing from *Hard-heartedness*

Feasting on
the Prayer of Examen

"The literal translation of the words 'pray always' is 'come to rest.'"

HENRI NOUWEN

"Prayer and love are learned in the hour when prayer has become impossible and your heart has turned to stone."

THOMAS MERTON

*I*f our heart is to be transformed from stone to flesh, we must place it in the path of God. And what better location for encountering God than prayer? It is in this uniquely intimate time that our defenses can be lowered and the walls we have put up around our hearts can be knocked down. Prayer is the sound of our voice, with God as the listener. Sometimes he hears whispers, and sometimes shouts. It is our most personal and tangible communication with our heavenly Father, and it can be done anytime, anywhere. Most importantly, prayer is a tool God uses for our transformation. While we pour out our words and thoughts before him and then sit in quiet receptivity, God softens our heart through the gentle prodding of the Holy Spirit. We must remind ourselves that this work of transformation is not our work, but God's. John Calvin said, "On the Sabbath we cease our work so that God can do God's work in us." Prayer is a portal to sabbath rest.

～·～·～

There are many forms and "ways" of prayer. There are prayers of confession, of adoration, and of supplication. There are prayers of relinquishment, of tears, and of despair. Prayers of gratitude, silent prayers, prayers of remembrance and expectation—each have their appropriate part in the prayer life of a person of faith. In particular, the Prayer of Examen is the prayer that most leads to softening a hard heart.

The Prayer of Examen is much what it sounds like. It is simply a time of inward personal examination. It is a tradition started by Ignatius of Loyola in the earliest part of the sixteenth century. He underwent a time of intense prayer and contemplation in a cave outside of a town in northeastern Spain called Manresa. Out of his reflections from this experience came his "Spiritual Exercises" and the Prayer of Examen.

Many adaptations are used today, but the goal of this prayer is personal examination of our day to discover where our lives intersect God's grace. They may be places of failure and hope, striving and surrender, anger and peace. In the Prayer of Examen, we honestly open ourselves to God in examination of our conscience, motives, desires, and actions.

In this place of prayer, we trust God to reveal to us knowledge about ourselves that empowers us to growth. This is not about obsessive introspection, but faithful and courageous surrender to a God whom we can trust. The God who wants to reveal the hardness of our heart will lead us to rest by softening it as we lay it before him.

When is the last time you sat in the presence of God and courageously laid open to him the places in your heart? If it has been a while, you may find this daunting and perhaps frightening. The hardness of your heart may have scarred over what was once an open and vulnerable relationship. Give yourself permission to sit still, and let God begin to make new again the things that have become hardened.

You may want to begin by asking God to reveal to you those times in your day when you were walking close to him, and the times when you were far away. Then, what were the things you were feeling during the faraway times? Was it anger, despair, fear, arrogance, a need for control, anxiety, impatience? How did any of these experiences lend to the hardening of your heart? When did you step back from God's presence and wooing? Don't be afraid of what surfaces. The God of the universe is not threatened by our frailty.

Next, as the Spirit gives you utterance, pray for God's grace to transform your heart. Ask him to give you courage for the next day, to keep you from hardening your heart in those same areas, to gently make you vulnerable to his moving in your life again. Use the words you are comfortable with—there is no official form. God knows your heart already, but it is important for you to speak what is in it so that you can hear it too. If we are not willing to be in honest and open relationship with our heavenly Father, our spiritual experience will be drained of life, and we will be tired from our hard-heartedness. The rest that gives refreshment to our spiritual life begins in this time of honest prayer.

These are the words I've used on occasion—perhaps they will help you to get started.

How is it that you know my name, God? Out of all the other too-many-to-number people that have come and gone, that will come and go, you somehow know my name.

Sometimes, lost in the immensity of life, a voice in me blurts out, "Know me." It isn't just because of a desire for significance. But because I don't even truly know myself, I want to know that somehow I am known.

But I recognize that if I am to be known by you, I'll have to give you access to all those places in me that are remote and unsettled. I will have to offer you my heart of stone. I don't always have the courage for that. While I want to know and be known, there are parts of me I don't know if I'm ready for you or me to see. Is it possible to sing with the psalmist, "Search me and know my heart, O God"? Is it safe to pray for a broken heart that can be re-formed by your touch?

It's possible that you will uproot the surface grass I've planted over the ugly dying thatch of my heart. And there I'll be, exposed and unmasked. A stone-hard patch of soil, too hard for anything to take root.

But Father, where else but here am I to know your grace? Help me to unclench my hands from my heart, to hold loosely the woman I think I am, to instead bravely reach for the woman you desire me to be.

And yes, Father, I want to be able to sing, even if softly, "Search me and know me." In that knowing, may I know you better and love you more completely.

In Jesus' name, amen.

Spiritual Rest Stops

Ceasing from hard-heartedness, feasting on the Prayer of Examen.

1. Empty the spiritual trash. Pray the prayer of confession. Acts 3:19 tells us to repent and return so that times of refreshing may be ours.

2. Dwell on the presence of God. Calvin Miller says that we enjoy the relaxed contemplation of God in what the early church fathers spoke of as *otium sanctum,* or "holy leisure." It is only in this "holy leisure," free from the busyness and cares of an overbusy schedule, that we can truly enter a deeper communion with Christ.

3. Make a "kneeling prayer" pillow. Sometimes it helps facilitate our times of prayer to have a "prop" or "tool." I made my pillow out of heavy cotton and filled it with sand. Then I made an outer, more decorative cover from a lovely tapestry. The pillow is portable, and it gives me a "place" for praying.

4. When words won't come, pray the prayer Christ taught his disciples. The Lord's Prayer covers our past ("forgive us our debts"), our present ("give us this day our daily bread"), and our future ("lead us not into temptation").

5. Take refuge in the intimate rest of prayer. Richard Foster writes in his book on prayer, "For too long we have been in a far country: a country of noise and hurry and crowds, a country of climb and push and shove, a country of frustration and fear and intimidation. And he welcomes us home: home to serenity and peace and joy..." God invites us out of the noise and out of our self-consumption to rest—rest in the intimacy of prayer. Pray sentence prayers, or heart-emptying prayers. Use forms from liturgy and church tradition, or words you have carefully composed. Be spontaneous or organized. Somewhere along the way, the Holy Spirit will mature your childlike petitions into a disciple's time of communion.

Ceasing from
the Need to Know Everything

Feasting on Mystery

"A man can accept what Christ has done without knowing how it works; indeed, he certainly won't know how it works until he's accepted it."

C.S. LEWIS

"Ever since the Garden, we have been indiscriminate suckers for the enticement of omnipotence. We are cerebral voyeurs, unable to accept the idea that some knowledge may lie outside our legitimate purview....We want to be able to 'prove God' so that everyone can really know and quit worrying—especially us. God demands active faith; we seek irrefutable certainty."

JAMES SENNETT

All of the drywall patching and sanding was finally finished. As the last bit of dust fell to the hardwood floor, the rollers came out and swathed the patches in primer. The preparation was complete now. I would have to choose a color.

I had been avoiding this decision because, frankly, I just don't really like color on walls. I enjoy it in your house, but in my house colored walls make me tired. But it just seemed a shame to do all that work and leave the walls the same old white they had always been. It's sort of like getting a haircut and no one noticing that you got one. But white is what I like, and I suppose there's nothing wrong with that. I used to worry about the lack of color in my home and the clothes in my closet, but when I read Georgia O'Keefe's biography, "I" started to make sense to me. She dressed in only black and white because she said having color around her made choosing colors on her canvas more difficult. I am a painter, and so that must be my story. It actually makes sense to me, and I know that I find gallery walls relaxing and contemplative—and they are always white. I was quite sure that I would once again pick white for my walls.

Do you know what "white" means? Aside from the dictionary's informative "the achromatic color of maximum lightness," I had always thought it was just basically the absence of color. So when my painter sent me to the paint store to pick out my color, I went with no apparent anxiety since I would just be picking "white."

When was the last time you went to the paint store? Because I'm just going to tell you that it was not what I was prepared for. Each brand of paint had its own display under "color-correct" lighting, and the little color swatches fanned east to west in perfectly ascending and descending hues. A mosaic of tints assaulted my no-color sensibility, and I almost feigned interest. But the pragmatist in me spoke up and said to the paint man, "Yes, I'd like a can of white paint."

As I look back on it now, I see that what I thought was a quirky smile on his face was more likely an "Are you kidding, lady?" smirk. He took me to the "whites" section where all of the little square shades, tints, and hues of warm or cold white stood like peg teeth waiting to be pulled.

I explained to the man again that I simply wanted plain old white paint, and he reluctantly told me about contractor white #977. That should have settled it. I should have been done. I should never have walked over to the "white" section again, but I did. I just wanted to make sure that with all of those non-colors, I was getting the non-color I liked best.

I came home with six quarts of white paint. Eggshell, antique lace, milk, parchment, pearl, and linen. It was instantly clear that linen was too brown and pearl too pink, but the others fell into far more subtle shades of unacceptability. Another trip to another paint store and another three quarts of white paint later, there was still no acceptable white to be found. My walls were spotted with dirty whites, yellow whites, bright whites, and new whites. All unsatisfactory. Any one of the whites would probably have suited me fine, but in the context of so many, *none* seemed right. Finally I went to a small area of wall that still had some of the old color of white. It was like finding an old friend. It was familiar, safe, and not too white. That was the best white. I loved that white. Why couldn't I just have that white?

I called my painter to see if he had a record of what we had used before, and after some searching he called me back. Contractor white #977.

In the profusion of options my senses had left me. It was inconceivable to settle for something so homogenized as contractor white #977, with so many other more well-packaged choices. I mean, what kind of name is that? "Milk" and "sun-bleached sand" sound so much more charming. It was as if I could not know #977 to be right until I had answered all my questions about the others.

Overthinking things is a habit I have developed with much practice. But sometimes you have to be content to accept something even without knowing everything about it. Knowledge and wisdom are not bad things—in fact the Scripture shows them to be highly prized possessions. But a relentless need to know borders on a need to control, which borders on a trip to the tree of the knowledge of good and evil.

Of all the trees in the garden, Adam and Eve were forbidden access to only one: the tree of the knowledge of good and evil. With all I have read by theologians wiser than me, I am convinced that this tree could have been any tree. It could have been the tree of "youth" or "great skill," and the point would still be the same. They were forbidden to eat from one tree. It was a matter of obedience. The trees were not magical trees but sacramental trees, as Old Testament scholar Derek Kidner points out. They were a physical means for a spiritual transaction. They were the opportunity for God's creation to be confronted with his will and to respond.

The command not to eat of that tree was not given because God was afraid Adam and Eve would become as smart or all-knowing as he. Rather, it was to set in motion the concept that *God* is the decider of right and wrong. The fact that the *kind* of the tree supports that concept makes the lesson all the more poignant. It was not so much *what* they ate but *that* they ate. They wanted to be in control, and God said he was in control. Eve's unbridled curiosity rejected the knowledge of God for the knowledge of his creation. That is where the shalom was broken.

I know there are times when I overthink things to the point of trying to be in obsessive control. Picking paint is inconsequential to my soul's health, but overthinking the likelihood that God's grace will redeem me might not be.

The part of me that is Eve's descendent becomes obsessed with the need to know things, and I can end up frustrated and in a heap. There are some things that just "are," and I don't need to know more. It should be enough that God has said he loves me. I don't need to overanalyze how and why.

Please do not take me as saying that we should not acknowledge the intellectual side of our faith. I believe we should be thinking people of faith. But there are some things that must be simply accepted without our completely understanding or knowing. In 1 Corinthians 13 we read that now we see in a mirror dimly, but then we will see face to face. We only know in part now, but then we will know fully, as we have been fully known. There are some things I won't know, no matter how hard I think about them. But the promise is not just that one day I will know, but that even now, I am fully known. I may not know myself or comprehend the abstract conundrums of faith, but God knows me and understands all. I am not set loose, untethered, in the universe with my unknowing. God continues to hold me.

How is God both immanent and transcendent, near and far, here and there? What is the origin of evil? What is the proper tension between predestination and free will? What about the virgin birth, the incarnation, and the resurrection?

It is good to ask these questions and to wrestle with them—to a point. But at some point you begin to move from faith to wanting to be in control. Ours is a dynamic faith, not a static one. We move in and out of knowing, but faith holds us. But if you find that you are obsessed with doubts and plagued by fears of unknowing, you are probably sitting at the base of the tree. And though the fruit looks enticing and you may consider reaching for it, you need to hear the voice of God say to you, "You are known, and I know." To be known by the One who knows the answers to the questions that shake your soul should curb your fruit-craving. And it can give you rest from the consuming need to know.

Ceasing from *the Need to Know Everything*
Feasting on *Mystery*

*"The morbid logician seeks to make everything lucid and
succeeds in making everything mysterious.
The mystic allows one thing to be mysterious,
and everything else becomes lucid."*

G.K. CHESTERTON

*"We live in a time when faith is thin, because our aching
for what is above and beyond us has been anesthetized
and our capacity for wonder reduced to clever tricks."*

ALAN JONES

*"We cover our deep ignorance with words, but we are
ashamed to wonder, we are afraid to whisper 'mystery.'"*

A.W. TOZER

We have had three weeks of unrelenting rain
and gloom, and I am beyond weary of
wiping muddy dog paws. Jim has become
proficient at giving them toe-baths, while I have been on
cleanup duty on our hardwood floors. The once white
towels are now a dingy shade of soil. The backyard has
been unkindly turned over in the process of construction

this year, and we have come to know the underside of our lawn. A small section of our fenced-off, secured piece of real estate has been affectionately dubbed Lake Thomas. As the water has pooled outside, I have furtively watched for signs of leaks in our ten-year-old roof, fearful of the water's unrelenting pursuit of the inside of my nest. But it would seem we are to escape leaks, enduring only the mud and its lack of manners.

I could honestly not have told you if it was nine in the morning or four in the afternoon by looking out my windows. For a while I enjoyed the cloistering effect and cozied up with blanket and spiced cider. But the romance quickly faded, and I slipped into a mildly catatonic state of nonengagement with the weather. Productivity came in stops and extremely-discipline-induced starts, and my grumpiness ripened.

But in the quiet shadow of those passing weeks, the leaves on the trees were busy exchanging summer green for the chroma of fall. And today their beauty has been exposed under the sparkle of sunlight. All things have become new again. The mud has passed away, the dry ground has come. My soul unfolds, and I sing again of the *mysterium fidei*, the mystery of faith.

Nature is so faithful to lead us behind the curtain of heaven for glimpses of the "something else" that denies words. In the moments when I am caught by beauty, I am once again aware of the mysteries that defy conventional empirical knowing. The times when I am most aware of the goodness of God are when the light seems brightest, the colors most intense. But it is in these transforming encounters with mystery, that the mud that has annoyed me for weeks becomes seeable as God's medium of choice on occasion.

Kierkegaard has said that in matters of faith, the only difference between the simple and the wise is that the simple don't understand, and the wise understand that they don't understand. Our faith is a wonderful combination of knowable and unknowable, of verities and mysteries. While there is much to be known through the rational approach of reasoning and apologetics, sometimes we are afraid to simply rest in the transforming beauty of mystery. The incarnation, the resurrection, the Holy Spirit, heaven, and salvation can all be unsettling mysteries of faith.

We must begin with the fact that God has revealed himself in creation and the person of Christ, and that he desires to be known. He is unknowable in the sense that we can't know all, but he is knowable in the sense that he is a personality who chooses to interact with his creation. He is perhaps unknowable in essence and predictability, but we are assured in the Gospels that for those who would seek, he desires to be found.

These abstractions may seem irrelevant until we are caught between life and death by uncertainty. It is in those times that we learn how finite are the lenses through which we see from this side of heaven. But in our uncertainty, God is faithful to reveal himself even in the scraps of mystery. In our existence we see his imprint of presence.

In our post-Enlightenment hunger for empirical certainty, we must remember to rejoice in the things we can only stand in awe at. Wonder is sometimes viewed as romantic and childish in comparison with the notion that all true knowledge is material and quantifiable. And that is when we lose the possibility of revelation, epiphany, and whispers from heaven. I'm certainly not saying we should disregard logic, precision, or reason. But I am saying that in those times when we cannot put words to what we feel, be it good or bad, there is an unknowable mystery that embraces us. We must embrace back.

Living this side of heaven, our longing for certainties will have to be satisfied with partial glimpses. In *God in the Dock,* C.S. Lewis describes looking at a beam of light in a dark shed. When looking at the light, he could see dust particles floating and the contrast of light with darkness. He was seeing the beam. Then he moved his eyes so that the beam was in them. He didn't see the toolshed or the beam, but he saw leaves and a tree outside the shed, and the sun 90-odd million miles away. This was, he said, the difference between looking at the beam and looking along the beam. Mystery leads us to sometimes be satisfied with looking along the beam.

We are body, soul, and mind. If we do not encounter our faith with all three, we fracture what was intended to be whole. With our body we sense the world around us, with our soul we encounter it, with our mind we understand it. We can use the tools of fiction, imagination, nature, art, and beauty. Their capacity to embody meaning and communicate truth can unravel the mysteries of the incarnation and help us to look along the beam.

So we must feast on mystery, and not fear what we cannot know. Without mystery we would be hollow creatures without vocabulary for wonder and with no capacity to enter into the majesty of creation. We must settle in our minds once and for all that "seeing is believing" is not good enough for the person of faith. Hebrews 11:1 says, "Faith is the assurance of things hoped for, the conviction of things not seen." This is the essence of the balance between known and unknown, faith and reason, verities and mysteries, restlessness and rest.

Spiritual Rest Stops

Ceasing from the need to know everything, feasting on mystery.

1. Relinquishing control is an exercise that must be repeated. Our desire to know and be known is normal and rational, but moving to a place where we cannot make peace with what is out of our control is unhealthy. There is a Quaker tradition of placing your hands out in front of you, palms facing up. When you feel you have placed your thoughts before the Lord, you turn your palms down, symbolizing that you no longer hold what was in them. Use this simple act when you are beginning to assume control again and need to relinquish it.

2. Plant a scatter garden of unknown "mixed" seeds. Nurture and feed the young plants and patiently wait to see what they will become. Not knowing exactly what you have planted will help you experience the joy of mystery in the growth season, and then the joy of discovery in the blooming season.

3. Finish this sentence: "If I could know anything, I would like to know..." Now, imagine that you have the answer to your wondering. How would you live your life any differently? Do you really need to "know" in order to live your life in that new way?

4. Purchase multiflavored candy when you go to your next movie. Enjoy the surprise of each new flavor in your mouth as you select a piece of candy in the dark. Not knowing what flavor comes next will help teach you to relax in the adventure of each new bite.

Ceasing from *Anxiety*

Feasting on *Peace*

"Worry does not empty tomorrow of its sorrow,
it empties today of its strength."

Corrie ten Boom

"Every tomorrow has two handles. We can take hold of it
with the handle of anxiety or the handle of faith."

Henry Ward Beecher

*J*im was going out of town for three days. I won-
dered how my mother did it all those years
when Dad was stationed on a ship in the ocean
for months at a time. Jim and I had rarely slept apart from
each other in the 20 years of our marriage, and I was not
used to being home alone. I was grateful for the two
schnauzers who would be with me, but they weren't
exactly trained German Shepherd police dogs.

I planned things carefully. I was looking forward to the
quiet of my time alone, but I was just the slightest bit
uncomfortable. I scheduled dinner out with a friend one
evening and arranged for the friend to come by my house
and pick me up. That way I would not have to go from the
car to the front door by myself after dark. Once safely

inside, I had projects to occupy my time. I sewed a skirt and organized the taxes. On my outing on Saturday, I had a stereo installed in the car as a surprise for Jim.

On the first night, I came home after dinner and waved to my friend as she watched me safely into the front door. I worked on my skirt and the taxes until after midnight and then went upstairs to try to sleep. I knew it would be the time when all the lights were out and the house was stilled that I would be the most anxious. So I devised some plans for putting my mind at ease. Of course I set the house alarm. After that, I went through our 1920s cottage closing all of the doors to the many rooms. There is a long hallway that leads to the master bedroom, and I closed all of the doors to the other rooms leading off of it. The house has hardwood floors and nine-foot-high ceilings, causing even the slightest sound to echo throughout. My logic was that if someone managed to break into the house without the alarm going off or the schnauzers barking, I would hear them coming because they would have to open the doors to get to me. Of course, if I had seen this in a movie, I would have been smugly laughing at the insanity of this woman's reasoning.

Perhaps it was too many movies that brought me to such embarrassing behavior in the first place.

Anyway, my brilliant security plans had just begun. Next, I shut the bedroom door and jammed a chair under the doorknob. Then I got a pair of shoes that are easy to slip into and set them under the window by my bed. I put the large flashlight under my bed so I could break the window for quick egress (that's security talk for exiting the building). I put an empty pillowcase by the shoes to put the dogs in and lower them out the window. My last counter-intruder measures were inspired by an untested theory: I put a can of hair spray along with a lighter on my bedside table to use as a torch, a sort of deterrent—a distraction to buy me time to break the window, grab the dogs, and escape.

After successfully readying my security measures, I lay my head down between the two dogs and fell fast asleep. I was surprised and relieved to wake up eight hours later after a solid night's sleep, with no encounters to report. The dogs followed me through the house, undoing the preventive steps I had devised the night before. The first thing I noticed was the chair I had securely placed under the doorknob of my bedroom door—a door that opened "out." This meant that the only person the chair would have hindered would have been me trying to get out of the bedroom. Anyone attempting to come in would have suffered no more than a chair falling at their toes. Next I turned off the security system and began opening all of the other doors with a subtle smile on my face, evidence of the pride I felt at taking such good care of myself on this, my first night alone. Well, you know what they say pride cometh before. I put my tennis shoes on and decided to take a morning walk. When I opened the front door, I found my keys swinging freely in the outside of the lock.

In one very small second, all of my antics of last night passed before my eyes, and I instantly pictured God in heaven, smiling with his God-hands on his God-hips and saying, "I will take care of you." All of my efforts at protecting myself were worthless with my keys hanging right there in the front door. Similarly, the keys to our anxieties are hanging right on the outside of our hearts, and yet God still guards those hearts.

Anxiety comes in two distinct forms: specific and general. Anxieties about heights, close spaces, reptiles, and death are specific forms of anxiety. And there are multiple forms of specific anxiety disorders. These are certainly rest thieves, but they are not the ones I want to address here. Those forms of anxiety and panic disorders are acute and must be addressed by qualified health professionals. The type of anxiety that I want to challenge us to cease from is the more general type. It is a state of uncertainty about something in the future, or the future itself—the "what ifs."

I was a victim of the tyranny of the "what ifs" that night. What if someone breaks in, and the alarm doesn't work, and the dogs don't hear, and I must escape, and so on, and so on. When we wind ourselves up into "what ifs," we sacrifice reason for anxiety and start down a path of self-defeat. Our imagination feeds our feelings of vulnerability, and our sense of power is diminished. Our general anxiety that something negative could happen in the future becomes the thief of our rest.

There is a certain amount of "worry" that spurs productivity. Some jobs depend on the skill of worry. And there is nothing wrong with the efficiency brought on by anticipating potential problems. But at some point, worry becomes toxic, and we become exhausted.

Fearing the worst, expecting and maintaining a vigil for bad news or disaster, imagining what could go wrong, and in general having a morbid preoccupation with the future, is nothing other than surrendering our rest to anxiety. Speculating on the bad things that might happen is not necessarily unhealthy, but obsessing over them is. A Swedish proverb says, "Worry gives a small thing a big shadow."

When we allow our minds to wander into "what if" territory, they become locked in a position of negativity, and we can't think reasonably. When I speak to large groups, I sometimes find myself fixating on one face in the crowd that doesn't seem to be tracking with me. Five hundred faces can send me the "good job" look, but one can cause me to worry for days that I didn't do a good job. What if I wasn't humorous enough, or challenging enough, or relatable? I remember being at an event once when I had a run in my stockings, and I worried the entire time that no one would hear what I had to say because they would be staring at my leg, appalled at the run in my hose. What if they think I am a slob and don't respect my ability to speak on the topic effectively? Worry and "what if" stole my ability to rest.

Many times, our "what ifs" are sourced in feeling insignificant or out of the loop. Sometimes we are afraid of failure or of being judged unjustly. But this general form of anxiety I am referring to all comes back to a desire to be in control. We are sensitive creatures subtly preoccupied with our frailty, and this leads us to anxious thoughts.

Our children get sick, our parents' health fails, our spouse feels pressure in his chest, we find an out-of-place lump, and...our anxiety meter pegs. Employees are laid off, our job performance wanes, and new talent threatens us. People we thought were our friends betray or ignore us. We long to be in control of our days, our successes, and our reputations. Dear friend, we aren't. But God is reliable. He is in control. And this is the news that should set us ceasing from anxiety.

In both the sermon on the mount (Matthew 6:25-34) and the sermon on the plain (Luke 12:22-31) Christ directs us not to worry. The Greek word for worrying used here is *merimnao*. It is a verb that points to being negatively troubled about the future. Jesus gently points out our error in thinking that we can secure our own future, or even provide for our daily needs by ourselves. He confidently opens the passage with the instruction, "Do not worry about your life." And then he uses the beautiful pictures of how the birds are fed and the flowers of the field are clothed, and knowingly asks, how could we worry about such things if God so diligently cares for sparrows and transitory flowers? And, he reasons, how can worrying add time to your life? This message should open our eyes to the irony of our thinking we were ever in control to begin with.

Worry, anxiety, a struggle to be in control—all these will steal our rest. They are such insidious habits that they will even invade the small patch of rest we *do* fence off, if we are not vigilant. Our vigilance is sourced in knowing this: Even when we have done all we can do to secure our lives, it is still God who protects us anyway. All of our plans and efforts are insufficient to save us. The keys are always hanging in our front doors, and it is only his faithful hand that keeps us secure.

Ceasing from *Anxiety*

Feasting on *Peace*

*"I rest beneath the Almighty's shade,
My griefs expire, my troubles cease;
Thou, Lord, on whom my soul is stayed,
Wilt keep me still in perfect peace."*

CHARLES WESLEY

*"The LORD bless you and keep you; the LORD make his face
shine upon you and be gracious to you; the LORD turn his
face toward you and give you peace."*

NUMBERS 6:24-26 NIV

*"Perhaps the human lesson is always submission. We
have a choice: to rebel or to recognize our powerlessness
while maintaining our faith."*

ANNE TRUITT

I served my term in the nursery of our small church recently. There were two of us fully grown women and four children under the age of three. But even with such a small group, there were too many crayons to be eaten, too many chairs to fall off of, and too many of "them" and not enough of "us." It was frightening and exhausting. I was a nervous wreck from the moment the mothers and fathers left. I feared for the little lives with the introduction of each new activity. We tried a Bible story, during which Harrison preferred to crawl over the table. We tried coloring, and Sam tried to eat the yellow ochre crayon. During snack time, I feared they would all choke on grapes, and tiny Olivia was in danger of being rolled over by my large chair as I leapt to block a miniature finger from going into an electrical outlet. And throughout all of our activities, Jacob quietly but persistently requested that we watch "Veggie Tales."

Just before the end of our hour-and-a-half together, I found a magical bottle in the toy box. It seems that when a thin skin of liquid soap is stretched over the plastic outline of a circle on the end of a stick and blown, life is good. Bubbles. We blew and chased bubbles for ten glorious minutes. We took turns blowing, and all of us pursued the bubbles, trying to catch them on our small, fat, short, long, and skinny fingers. Little puffy palms were raised upwards to the sky. Giggling that began in the purest of hearts consumed the room, along with tiny, sloppy puddles of liquid where once were floating orbs. I looked over and saw Olivia reaching and stretching, begging the bubbles to visit her hands, when all along she carried a hitchhiker bubble on the back of her shoulder. The delicate spheres would not be caught, but they lighted where they chose to.

***

This bit of time outside my comfort zone had once again surprised me with the profound blessing of heaven. In a season of all-consuming anxiety and worry, God had reminded me that his peace rests on me. I can't chase it down or manufacture it, but God has promised me that his peace, which goes beyond my understanding, will keep my heart and mind. Peace rests on those who rest in God. Shalom—that state of wholeness, completeness, and wellness—is ultimately the gift of a loving heavenly Father.

In the Gospel of John, Christ tells us, "Peace I leave with you; my peace I give you. I do not give to you as the world gives. Do not let your hearts be troubled and do not be afraid" (14:27 NIV). The word used for "troubled" is *tarasso* in the Greek, and it means "to be disquieted, or restless." As we pursue rest, we will have to cease from our anxieties, cease from being disquieted, and rest in the peace of God. There is no rest that satisfies the soul like the peace of God. As Augustine prayed, "We are restless, until we find our rest in Thee."

I remember the particular day several years ago when it came to me that all the things I was pursuing were like those little bubbles that would not be caught. I had career goals and peer-approval goals that haunted me and drove me to a point of consuming distraction. With every expectation that was disappointed, my heart became more disquieted and troubled. On the other hand, the accomplishments and accolades that came my way were never satisfying enough. There was always someone more talented, more creative, and more loved than I was, and so I felt that I had to produce more and strive harder.

On my day of personal epiphany, I was sitting on a small love seat that I had covered in layers of mosquito netting, and the sun was bleaching the already white walls in the room until they glowed. The muscles in my body unwound, and I sat, not in my usual curled-up, knees-to-my-chest position, but with legs stretched out and arms east and west. The puddles from unattained bubbles that had been my plans sparkled as they dried in the sun, and the precious bubble of God's peace rested on my back. The unbelievable release came when I realized that all I really wanted in my life was to feel the peace of God, and it quieted the restless striving that had robbed me of shalom. Christ promised a peace, not as the world gives—which was what I had been pursuing—but a peace that passes understanding.

~ · ~ · ~

I suppose it shouldn't surprise me, in this advent season in which I write, that God chose to use children to further my understanding of peace.

Last night I was ruminating on this subject, struggling with how to contain in words what is so elusive in experience. We went to hear our friends' children sing in their school Christmas program. Brette and Michael performed confidently with their classmates in various states of holiday dress. Each had their moments to shine. At one point, 44 children in white shirts, boys with red suspenders and girls with colorful sashes, delicately sang out Christmas declarations of silent nights and ringing bells. Attentive children and a loving teacher–director with long red fingernails ushered in the tidings of comfort and joy. Moms dressed in puffy holiday sweaters saved seats for late dads who hurried straight from work and squeezed into rows that were designed to comfortably hold fewer people. Nervous parents mouthed the words of the songs with their children. And at last, a curly-haired fourth-grade boy recited, in a "Charlie Brown Christmas" voice, "At Christmas, we receive God's gift of Jesus. That is what peace is all about."

Perhaps we can find peace only when our hearts have been ploughed up and turned over enough to receive the gift of Christ. Not only in the moment of salvation, but in the everyday events that can plant either worry or peace. Our Lord has not flippantly promised us peace without being aware that we will be challenged with troubles. In John chapter 16, he tells us there will be times of trouble in the world, but he assures us that the world is his and all that is in it, and he promises peace. I'd like to be able to tell you how to attain peace in five easy steps, but the truth is, more likely than our being able to work our way into peace, it will come to us in ways beyond our understanding or machinations. But I do offer some helpful ideas to place you in the path of peace, to help put your heart in a disposition to receive it.

First, we must recognize that we will encounter times when we will have to surrender control. This is the first step to ceasing from anxiety and feasting on peace. It is the most elemental, and yet highest-impact, action we can take in our pursuit of rest. Illness, disappointment, rejection, betrayal, loss of means, and broken hearts are all a part of the package of life. If we don't settle with ourselves that we cannot control these things, we will not even begin to know personal peace.

Secondly, we have to remind ourselves that even though we have relinquished control, we are not sent untethered into life's anxious circumstances. God still secures our tether, and he is still in control. None of the expected or unexpected storms we encounter are surprises to our heavenly Father.

Remember the story in the Gospels about the disciples being at sea and encountering a massive storm? This was not a slight squall—the Greek word used here indicates a "seismic" storm. When they rushed to wake Jesus in the back of the boat, they said, "Lord, don't you know that we are perishing?" Have you ever been in the middle of your own personal storm and felt that Jesus might perhaps be asleep? Notice that early in this story Jesus himself told the disciples to set sail in that boat, at that time. He knew full well what was ahead, but all along he wanted to remind them that he was in control, even of unexpected storms. He spoke one word to the storm—"peace"—and the waves were stilled and the rains ceased. Immediately.

Our storms are not always immediately silenced, but our anxieties can be. We can know that we don't have a sleeping, unaware Savior who is caught off guard by our circumstances. He is fully aware, and fully in control, and speaks to us this word: "peace."

So we relinquish our control, recognize that God is in control, and we do what we can do. You see, doing these first two things does not mean that we just sit back and let life's storms blow us where they will. We still do what we can. But the idea of feasting on peace reminds us that when we get to the part we can't do anything about, we release the worry. The disciples still continued to sail their boat and fight the storm as best as they could with all of their fishermen skills, but ultimately they surrendered to Christ's ability to save them. So we should use what skills and abilities we have to deal with our anxieties, as best as we can, and then we surrender the rest to God.

⌒ · ⌒ · ⌒

I would like to suggest two more tools to put us in the path of peace. In a calm moment, begin to address the things you have great fear about. If you have a fear about your financial provision, one day, after you have successfully paid the bills, begin to imagine your worst fear concerning money. Allow yourself to picture the absolute worst—and then remind yourself that God has cared for the needs of the lilies in the field, and he will care for you in his time and his way.

In perspective of eternity, what is the absolute worst that can happen to you? When we are promised heaven, the "worst thing that can happen" begins to lose its ability to stress us. Surrender to the fact that God's time and way may not be the time and way you want (this is the part where you relinquish control), and then trust that he will rescue you. What this will specifically look like in your life is a picture yet to be drawn, one that is known only in the mind of God. But the peace comes in realizing that whatever the worst possible scenario may be, God has promised to never leave us or forsake us. If this sounds purely spiritual and not very practical, don't be fooled. Until we deal with our anxieties and lack of rest in a spiritual form, any other rest will be short-lived. The point of God's peace, God's rest, is that it is a spiritual approach that produces long-lasting practical results.

The last suggestion I would like to present is to find yourself a safe haven. This is a spouse, friend, relative, or group of any of the above whom you trust to desire your highest good. Your safe haven should be a person or two you can count on to never betray your heart. It will be a small place, but a safe place—one that breeds and nurtures peace.

My next turn in the nursery is not for several more weeks. In the meantime, I am working on these things myself. I am relinquishing control—and remembering that that doesn't leave me vulnerable, at the whim of the universe. God is reliably in control. I am doing what I can about the things that produce rest-draining anxiety in my life. I am also, in my sane moments, facing my fears and diffusing them by naming them. Fears are best diffused in the context of rest. And then, I am building my safe haven. I am writing the names of the friends and family who will not hesitate to step into my boat in the middle of a storm, who will be Christ enfleshed for me in my times of anxiety. Lastly, I will check our supply of bubbles and stock up. And I will prepare my heart to be spoken to, and peace to be given, in a place where I least expected it.

Spiritual Rest Stops

Ceasing from anxiety, feasting on peace.

1. Incorporate some form of regular Bible study into your daily life. You could perform all of the exercises in this book, but if you miss this one, you will never truly find rest. This is one of the best ways to get to know the God who promises to care for you. As you study, your confidence in him will grow, and your peace will multiply. You can purchase books to help you study. There are typical "devotional" books, but I have found a wonderful new world in, of all things, commentaries. There are commentaries on every book in the Bible, and they differ in character—academic versus devotional—from author to author. Make a realistic commitment to study Scripture, and you will begin to grow and flourish like the person described in Psalm 1 who delights in God's word. Self-help steps will begin to direct you, but Scripture study will sustain you.

2. What foolish anxiety stole your peace today? Annie Dillard said, "I meant to accomplish a good bit today. Instead I keep thinking: Will the next generations of people remember to drain the pipes in the fall? I will leave them a note."

3. Purchase a jar of bubbles. Go ahead. You have to do it. Blow them, chase them, observe them. In your play, allow God's peace to light on you.

4. Pray for God to give you the faith to live not in the "what ifs," but in the "even so's." The courage of Shadrach, Meshach, and Abednego said that if their worst "what ifs" came to pass, "even so" they would praise God. When you face those "what ifs" down, the perspective generated will bring the "ahh" of rest.

5. Use this exercise when you feel yourself drained of peace. Augustine has described heaven as "perpetual sabbath." This side of the curtain, begin practicing by truly entering sabbath rest. Peace will put you in a willing state of rest. Close your eyes and intentionally relax the muscles in your body. You will be surprised to discover that your shoulders, your stomach, your neck, and many places have been clenched tight with anxiety. Now, slow your breathing. You can do this while sitting at a red light or lying in your bed. I have begun to recognize my anxiety and its foolishness much more easily with this simple exercise.

Be spiritual sabbath rest for someone else.

"We must patiently learn to trust our heaviness, as a bird has to before he can fly."

RAINER MARIA RILKE

Is your spiritual campfire warm? If it is, then those standing outside in the cold will gather round. Vincent van Gogh said that if we believe in God, sooner or later someone will see the fire within us and come sit down. But he says we must be vigilant to tend this inner fire.

Aaron and Hur held up Moses' arms when he began to grow faint. Find *your* Aaron and Hur and offer to hold *their* arms up for a while.

Mail postcards to your "safe haven" people. Put a trust-building verse on them. Remind them that they are not alone, and thank them for being in community with you.

Spiritual rest is highly contagious. Pass the peace.

Breathing

"Breathe on me, breath of God;
Fill me with life anew…"

EDWIN HATCH

The package came with twelve crayon-colored latex balloons. It has been so long since I've had a need for balloons that I pull one out, and am amazed that such a tiny little teardrop shape can hold enough air to make it about the size of my head.

I start by stretching a red one. (I've been told this makes it easier to blow up.) I wrap my lips securely around the rolled edge and begin to deliver air. I find that if I will inhale deeply, I can exhale longer. The sides of the balloon expand as my lungs deflate. At the end of each breath, I am careful to tightly pinch the neck. Once, I didn't catch it quickly enough, and the air came flying out so fast I couldn't save it. The air spilled out—and for a moment, I mourned the loss of my life-sustaining breath that was escaping so frivolously.

Somehow, in this exercise of the balloon, I am thinking of sabbath-keeping. Of course, this isn't terribly hard to believe as I have been thinking about sabbath rest now for months. I have begun to find it everywhere. Those Exodus verses that continually invite us to sabbath rest also invite us to refreshment. The Hebrew word for refreshment here is actually *naphash,* meaning "to breathe." So as I donate a breath from my own body to the balloon, I am experiencing the rhythm and refreshment of breathing.

***

I have been particularly aware of the essential qualities of breathing this year, as my parents have both been diagnosed with pulmonary problems. Typically, the life-giving oxygen we take for granted is efficiently piped into our bodies without our even having to consciously think about it. But when disease and sickness threaten that process, we become acutely aware of the minute-to-minute functions our bodies perform, and what a fragile state they actually exist in. And nothing is quite as "every minute" as breathing. We trust our bodies to do their job and function as they were intended. Rhythmically refreshing us with each breath.

The rhythm of breathing is composed of two parts: inhaling and exhaling. The work of inhaling is completely balanced by the response of exhaling. With each breath taken, air moves down the windpipe into the bronchial tubes and eventually into the lungs, where the alveoli transfer oxygen into the bloodstream. The two parts of breathing are designed to maximize oxygen intake and waste removal. It is almost frightening to consider that in each inhale we take in not only life-sustaining oxygen but some 250 different volatile substances. When we exhale, carbon dioxide and other toxins are eliminated. Without the inhale, we would suffocate; without the exhale, we would be poisoned. It takes the rhythmic functioning of inspiration and expiration for healthy function. And it is in the delicate balance of the two parts that we are refreshed.

In much this same way, we are invited to be physically and spiritually refreshed, as with a cool breeze or a breath

tioning of working and resting makes a complete breath.
When one of the two is out of balance, the rhythm is
thrown off and we don't receive the refreshment we long
for. You can only hold your breath for so long before
passing out—and on the other extreme, if you are
breathing too fast, you will hyperventilate and also pass
out. As I recognize my need for sabbath rest in my own life,
I see many cases where I have come close to passing out
emotionally, physically, or spiritually.

Gratefully, as my family has been told this year, there are
things we can stop doing that will maximize our breathing
health. One of the simplest things is to cease breathing
toxins that will damage the alveoli in our lungs and limit
oxygen absorption. These toxins are things like chemicals,
asbestos, or cigarette smoke.

"Toxins" threaten our experience of sabbath rest too.
Toxins to our sabbath rest are the things we have discussed
"ceasing from" throughout this book. They are the things
that keep us from experiencing the refreshment God offers
us. They are things that overload, overspend, and over-
consume our lives. And so we choose to cease from stress,
noise, negativity, numbness, and anger. We choose to cease
from busyness, hurry, overconsuming, and crowds. We
exhale fear, hard-heartedness, the need to know everything, and anxiety—all toxins to our rest.

We have discovered that not only are there things we
must cease from, there are things we can actively do to
improve breathing efficiency. There are actual exercises
one can perform that increase lung capacity and improve
pulmonary functioning. They allow more oxygen to be
delivered to the blood and more efficiently provide energy
for us to spend. It is not only in the cessation of some
things, but in the doing of others, that full breathing health
is experienced. Exactly as in our pursuit of sabbath rest.

199

And so in the same way that we deeply inhale oxygen, we inhale balance, silence, the positive, sensing, and flexibility. We breathe in deeply, trust, prayer, mystery, and peace. Exhaling, inhaling, ceasing, feasting, all in pursuit of *naphash,* a refreshing breath, sabbath rest.

⁓ · ⁓ · ⁓

All of this brings a new potency to the Old Testament story of Ezekiel's dry bones. From midway in chapter 36 of his book, Ezekiel has been communicating, through his apocalyptic visions, the good news of restoration. In this story, he uses the symbol of dry bones being restored to life. What better word picture could he have given us to communicate the mystery and wonder of redemption? What more appropriate picture would describe my over-spent life in need of rest? In verse five of chapter 37 he speaks the words of heaven: "This is what the Sovereign LORD says to these bones, 'I will make breath enter you, and you will come to life.'" If anything ever described my burned-out condition and need for sabbath rest, it is old, dry, dead bones. Bones that once held flesh and muscle teeming with life have become useless even to the scavengers of the desert.

Perhaps now you will consider pulling over into a rest stop. Gather up your dry bones, and take off your shoes. What can possibly restore our lives, refresh our spirits? What can put life back into these overspent bodies we try to exist in, these rattling dry bones? A breath. A breath from heaven. A sabbath breath.

To contact the author:
kimthomasbooks@comcast.net

For more information about Kim's other books,
Simplicity and *Living in the Sacred Now,* please
contact her at the above e-mail address.

Rest Thieves

Perhaps there are other rest thieves in your life that I haven't discussed in this book. Make a list and consider what you will need to "cease" from and "feast" on if you are to enter the rest God invites you to.

_____

_____

_____

_____

_____

_____

_____

_____

_____

_____

_____

_____

_____

_____

_____

_____

_____

_____

_____

_____

_____

_____

_____

_____

_____

_____

_____

_____

_____

_____

_____

_____

_____

_____

_____

_____

_____

_____

_____

Rest Thieves

A Vocabulary of Non-Rest

always: a statement of inflexibility

anxiety: misspent energy

bigger: a challenge to contentment

control: a state of being that misses out on surprise

counterfeit: temporary satisfaction

faster: the speed of striving

fear: a condition outside of trusting God

hurry: the pace of life that neglects wellness

instant gratification: the sacrifice of the valuable for the available

more: the place just past enough

must: the things that edge out "perchance"

never: a barrier to dreaming

now: a demand that eliminates the value of marinating in anticipation

striving: the opposite of resting

why: straining against the providence of God

worry: a chronic condition of needing to be in control

yes: sacrificing the important for the urgent

A Vocabulary
of Rest

balance: the right amount of this and that, of work and rest, of ceasing and feasting

bounty: seeing the most in what you already have

delight: enjoying what you do or have

enough: choosing contentment

genuine: finding the authenticity in life

goodness: God's stated value of sabbath time

gratitude: an attitude of seeing God's blessings

faith: trusting that God desires our highest good

investing: spending time on what is important rather than what is urgent

leisure: activity that doesn't have to be done

lingering: sitting in the moment

nap: a shameless activity of refreshment

no: a discerning refusal of busyness

patience: seeing the goodness in the appropriate passage of time

pause: the important time of renewal between activities

paying attention: reveling in the mysteries of creation

play: activity that does not contribute to the gross national product

pruning: removing distractions and dead weight

quiet: stilling the noises of life

relaxation: freedom from deadlines, appointments, and commitments

rhythm: the appropriate mix of work and play (see *balance*)

surrender: trusting that if you slow down you won't miss anything important

tranquil: the opposite of busy

trust: relinquishing control

vacation: a time of possibilities and discoveries

wealth: see *enough*

yes: the appropriate response to God's invitation to rest